HOW TO RAISE "PURFECT" KIDS

by

John Roy Bohlen

&

JOHN 5:30

THE KING'S INSTITUTE
THE CHURCH ON THE WAY

Printed in the United States of America.
Library of Congress Catalogue
Card Number 87-071522

ISBN 0-9607702-3-2

Published by, for and in behalf of the Kingdom of
God.
 Author and representatives may be contacted at:

GREAT COMMISSION MINISTRIES
P.O. Box 7123
Minneapolis, Minnesota, 55407, U.S.A.

Destiny Image Publishers
P.O. Box 351
Shippensburg, PA 17257
532-3040

The majority of the art in this book was done by the
Lord through the loving life of Becky Meyers.

Artwork taken from *How To Rule The World* was
done by Chris Wold Dyrud

HOW TO RAISE "PURFECT" KIDS

TABLE OF CONTENTS

PART II THE KEYS

Many Many Conversations. - 7. Have Everyone Take Notes. - 8. Remind Them That We Wrestle Not Against Flesh And Blood. - 9. Always Remain As Teachable As You Are Right Now. - 10. It Is Best To Not Counsel Alone. - Karen Has Some Thoughts -11. Teach Them To Express Gratitude For Each Other -12. Teach Them To See Each Other From God's Perspective. - 13. Teach Them The Power And Privilege Of Blessing. - 14. Share The Sacredness Of Celibacy. -15. Teach An Attitude Of Gratitude. - 16. Teach That We Can And Must Exercise Our Will Godward. - 17. Deal With The Myth Of Falling In Love. - 18. Define Fleshly, Soulish Or Spiritual. -19. Present A Formula For Dating, or "Mom's Talk By The Stairs". - Before The Marriage - 20. Never Conduct A Marriage That God Has Not Told You To. - 21. Never Minister To People On Their Terms, Or On Your Terms, But Only On God's Terms. - 22. Always Ask Each Of Them, "Is This Marriage The Perfect Will Of God?" "Are You Absolutely Sure?" -23. Teach Them That If They Are Married, That The Person That They Are Married To, Is Automatically The Perfect Will Of God, God's Perfect Choice For Them "Til Death, (or The Rapture) Do Us Part". - 24. Remember That The Only Thing Necessary To Make Any Relationship Work Is Total Commitment To The Will Of God. - 25. Destroy The Myth Of Falling "Out Of Love". - 26. The True Basis Of Love Is A Commitment Of The Will based On The Will Of God. - 27. Get Them To Agree That They Will Accept You As The Referee. - 28. The Withholding

INTRODUCTION

A Friend of mine walked into a book store, shook his head and said under his breath, "Waste of trees!" One day I asked my brother Michael what he thought of the book title, *HOW TO RAISE "PURFECT" KIDS.* He laughed heartily and said, "One thing's for sure. Folks will be lining up, willing to pay admission to see your kids!" We hope that you do have the opportunity to meet each of the children. But, for now, let me introduce the whole family to you!

ABOUT THE AUTHORS

John Roy Bohlen also has written a book on the most important thing in life, called *HOW TO RULE THE WORLD or SEEK YE 1st THE KINGDOM OF GOD.* John has also written a handbook for marriage entitled, *THE SEXUAL MINISTRY.* It is strongly recommended that you read these books. They can be ordered from your local bookstore, or from the address given on the back cover.

John received a B.A. from Bethel College in St. Paul in 1961 with a degree in philosophy and psychology. John and Karen were married after their graduation from Bethany Fellowship Training Center in 1964. He has worked as a farmer, bridge construction worker, shoe repairman, inventory counter, cook-ware salesman, counsellor, bus driver, concrete construction worker, roofer, probation officer, custodian, real estate salesman, fiberglass gunrunner, husband, father, evangelist, teacher, founder of churches and pastor and pastor to pastors.

John was a probation officer for Los Angeles County for 6 years, pioneered and pastored several city churches and has been counselling for more than twenty years. He and Karen and their four children, Joey, Kari, Dawn Joy and Joshua, travel extensively, singing and leading conferences and seminars on The Great Commission, Marriage and the Family, Church Growth and Renewal, Discipleship - Leadership Training, and Life Priorities.

JOHN'S EARLY CHILDHOOD

John Roy Bohlen was born June 27,1939 in Burlington, Iowa and first lived on Doemland Street. Half way through kindergarten, John and his family moved to an area southeast of New London, Iowa to the "Wesly Clarke farm", down the long unpaved lane where they "share cropped". The spot where the house and barn once stood is now an open field. After a couple of years, the family moved out to the main road to the "Becky Clarke" farm. While John was in the 3rd grade, the family moved to the "Row farm" southwest of Yarmouth, Iowa. There's an open field there, too, where the house once stood. Halfway through the 6th grade, John's parents Ruth, or 'Sonnie', and Roy purchased the old "Fox Farm" southeast of Prairie Grove, Iowa, so John, with his two older sisters Jolene and Sherrill, and his younger brother Michael and the folks all moved down the long lane, past the pump and the rock garden, past the orchard and the two barns, to the two story farm house.

What a place for growing up! Two hundred-forty some acres of sheer adventure! There were Indian burial mounds, a whole row of them. There was Flint River, some called it a 'crick', running through nearly two miles of the farm, past deep timber, flint bluffs from where the Indians used to get flint for their instruments. In the timber, there were gooseberries, mushrooms, hickory nuts, squirrels and quiet places. In the 'crick' there were fishin' holes, swimmin' holes and sometimes holes in the ice, which we skated around in the winter time.

There was work to do, also: Get water from the pump, slop the hogs, gather the eggs, fix the fence, get the cows, milk the cows, plowing, disking, harrowing, planting, cultivating, combining, shucking, raking, baling, gardening, spreading "bah-dur", cutting, sawing, splitting, hauling, stacking, starting and tending the fire, sitting on the oven door early winter mornings before we went to school.

Dad, wouldn't let us go barefoot in the spring time until the whipoorwill called.

On all of these farms, they never did have running water, unless John or somebody ran and got it. They drank their water from a dipper and bucket, and at potty time, there was the path out back to the two hole-er. All of the baths were either taken out back of the house using a small basin of water, or, when it was too cold outside, in a large galvanized wash tub in the house. Much of the time we had no electricity, and when we had a phone, it was an old crank'er. On our party line, we answered when it rang two longs and two shorts. Otherwise we sometimes just "listened in" to get the latest news.

It was two miles or so to the one room "Wild Cat" country grade school that sat on a hill in the woods. The road may be graveled by now...

KAREN

Karen Wold Bohlen, John's wife AND lover, has been a pastor's wife, a deaconess and prophetess, an officer in Women's Aglow, and has been a counsellor and speaker in the area of marriage and the family. She holds a degree as a Registered X-ray Technician, and also graduated from Bethany Fellowship in 1964. Their four children were all born "naturally", with John assisting as part of the birth team. Karen has assisted in other births as well, and has given training on prepared child birth, nursing, nutrition, parenting and the woman's ministry as a wife, lover and mother.

Karen is a "Proverbs 31" lady and definitely a "Kingdom Gutfighter". She would tackle hell with a bucket of water, and has. As Louis L'Amour says, "A woman fit to bear a race of warriors!" and "The kind to walk beside a man, not behind him!"

11

THE CHILDREN

Joey, seems like yesterday I could hold him in my 10″ hand. Until a "short" time ago he didn't seem to be growing as fast as he should, so I told him, "Joey, the day you get to be taller than your 6′1″ dad, I'll give you $100.00!" He took the challenge and has been growing like a weed ever since, coming up to 6′ 6″ and growing! He's in his second year at ORU. Bless you, Joey!

Kari has no enemies, except the Lord's, and many friends, a friend of God, - fun loving, serious and a prophetess. Go for it 'Kye'! Sweet spirit.

Dawn Joy sings in the madrigal group and choir as a senior in high school. She plans to attend a Christian College this fall. Precious lady, she's my friend!

Joshua has a righter spirit than any man I know, and seems like a younger version of the Old Testament Joshua. What a guy, 'Sesh'! Voted most valuable choir member, most talented, etc. At school, they asked him what he was high on, as he's always so full of enthusiasm for Life in the Lord. He answered, with face aglow, "I'm just high on the love of Jesus!!!" (By the way, the word "enthusiasm" comes from two Greek words, "in" + "Theos" or in God!)

YAHWEH YESHUA

The main Author, Jesus Christ, the Creator King of All the Universe, has some fabulous things to say here as well. After all, He created children and commissioned the raising of them. He intended and does intend that we be wonderfully successful in our raising of the children, so He has been given space here also. (satan can forget about asking for equal time. To hell with him, he's already had his say.)

QUESTIONNAIRE

INSTRUCTIONS & EXPLANATIONS:

Please do NOT put your name on this!!! (When using this questionnaire.)

Here are some of the reasons for this anonymous questionnaire: # 1. To help you; # 2. To help others; & # 3. To help us.

- teaching technique
- increased openness
- discover problem areas

Here's the reason we do not want you to sign this questionnaire. We want you to feel totally free to answer these questions without embarrassment, fear of discovery or shame. You may remain totally anonymous; in fact, we prefer that this be so, in order that you may have greater liberty in your answering. Please answer these questions to the best of your ability, without shame. If you have a question, please feel free to ask for assistance. We are also available to counsel with you about your deepest need or most secret problem. We have been successful in God in helping dear ones with condemnation, fears and "hang ups" from the past. Take your time with these questions, and let this be: A FUN ADVENTURE!

THE KING'S INSTITUTE
THE CHURCH ON THE WAY

1. Are you married?
2. If you have children, please give their ages & gender.
3. Do you think it is possible to raise "perfect kids"???
4. Do you think it is possible to live without sinning?
5. How many, if any, of your children were "unwanted mistakes"?
6. Please make a quick list of things you would do differently in your life, marriage & family, if you could do it over again.
7. Do you think that divorce is ever justified? If so, when?
8. Are any circumstances where abortion is justified?
9. Is a person ever justified for getting a wrong attitude?
10. Is one ever excused for holding a grudge, or bitterness or resentment toward anyone about anything?
11. Are you aware of any resentment or bitterness, within yourself, toward anyone?
12. About how many times do you have to tell your child(ren) to do something, before they will mind?
13. Do you spank your child(ren), when needed?
14. Are you willing to do anything God would tell you to?
15. If someone came up to you and asked how to be born again, what would you tell them? (explain how to be born again.)

16. Please guesstimate your spiritual temperture, on a scale between 0 - 100. (100 = razor-sharp and white-hot FOR GOD; 50 = luke-warm; 0 = sinful, undedicated and cold.)

17. How long have you been born again?

18. Have you ever read the Bible all the way through, without skipping any parts??? If so, about how many times?

19. Do you have any problems too deep or personal to tell anyone? Is there anything we can do to help?

20. Do you need confidential counselling about anything?

21. Please list 7 things in order of importance in your life.

22. Please list 5 of the most important things that Christ took of yours with Him to the cross.

23. How long have you been married?

24. Are you male or female?

25. Do you agree with this statement, "The only ingredient necessary to make any relationship work, is mutual and total commitment to the will of God."

26. Do you have any bitterness or unforgiveness toward your child or children or spouse?

27. Do you think you have need for inner healing from past hurts?

28. Were you a victim of incest, as a child? If so, by what relative(s)?

29. Were you a victim of child abuse, that is, were

you treated in a cruel manner by your parent or guardian?

30. Compared to all that you think that you should know about raising children, what percentage do you think you know?

31. What percent do you think the average Christian knows?

32. List things you would like to see changed about your mate.

33. Ditto — your children.

34. In your marriage, what percentage of the problems are your mate's fault?

35. Were you disciplined as a child? How? How often?

36. Did your parent(s) love you as a child? Did they tell you so? How often?

37. Are you a single parent?

38. List things you would like to see changed about your family life.

ACKNOWLEDGMENTS & DEDICATION

First of all, I want to thank the Creator King of all the Universe, Jesus Christ, Who reigns over all things and Who will reign forever and forever!!! I thank You Father God at all times and for every thing and in every circumstance!!!

In addition, I hereby do thank my fabulous wife! Thank you Karen for being the greatest mother in the world. Hasn't this been a "GREAT ADVENTURE"?

My darling children, thank you also! God's young man Joey, Joseph my first born, 4″ taller than my 6′1″, called to be a prophet and an apostle of God in the land, going forth to slay giants and dragons. Son, I'm so proud of you!

Kari Ruth, prophetess and precious one, full of life and joy, may your heart always be happy, and your spirit always be sweet! I know that this will be, as you abide in Christ!

Dawn Joy the prophetess-minstrel, may your voice be heard and your songs of praise be sung around the world, and beyond...

Joshua my precious prize winner for praise! May we always hear your prophet's worship. And God grant that you be as tall as Joey and as strong in Spirit!

18

To my mother Ruth (Sonnie) Vena Waters Bohlen Hussman, the greatest contralto in the world, and my greatest mommy! I cannot remember your ever having committed one sin, although you may have. Thank you for loving my dad and thank you for loving my Heavenly Father. And to you Edward for marrying my mother after my father died...Go on and fulfill an apostolic ministry, both of you.

To all who have interceded for us and for the ministry of Christ through us - Audrey, Karen and other unsung heroes: Thank You!!! We'll rejoice at your greater reward on The Day soon coming!

Special thanks to my dear artist friend who so sacrificially did the illustrations Becky Meyers and her husband Kenny, from McCook, Nebraska. Thanks also to Pastors Rob and Sherri Putz, Pastor David Perry, Brigitt and family from Albuquerque; Lyle Payne, family and church from Hastings, Ne.

Thanks again to David Turnidge and family for your sacrifice. You are a computer genius, and precious in God!

Thank you Robin Hansen, Denise Fleury, Beverly Hale, and especially, David and Cindy Purifoy, the St. Benedicts and each of you for your assistance at the computers, your sense of humor and sweet spirit has been an encouragement!

To Frank Mauer, Paul Was, John Mc Ginnitys, David Thompsons, Al, Kerry & Denise Smith, Audrey, the Carpenters, Rundles, Savageaus, Ferris, Wolfbauers, Betty Webster, Ron Green, Fogartys, Shackeltons, Taylors, Paul Hegstrom, Larry & Georgia

Hayes & boys, George Kramers, Agnes, Darrell & Susie Pughs, the Stoekels, Dr Bob Smith, Bethel College, Bethany Fellowship, Bistlines, Louis L'Amour, the Garborgs, John, 700 Club-Love Lines, my brother Michael Bohlen and Sandy, Bruce & Brenda; Fleurys, Souehls, Julie Duerr, Bob Hanson, David Ophaug, the lovely Robert Benedicts, Doug and Ginny Johnson, Kevin Pound, Roy Lucas, the Gary Dodge family, L.D., Ruth Stapleton, Noel Garzia, Beverly Hale, Beverly Jorgenson, Ralph Spezio, Bistlines, Grinsteads, Gene & Francis Walker family; the Bob Carlins, Catherine Higgins, Maloneys, Mel Baileys, Son of Righteousness Ministries, Lady St Josephine, Alan Langstaff, St.s Cameron & Anna Simmons, Sid Roth, Charles & Glad Trombley and to each of you, our friends, who have been our friends, and who have proved your friendship time after time!

Pastor Chuck and Judy Dodge, thank you!!!

Thanks to a team of people who have prayed for us and who have contributed financially to the ministry.

Thanks to all of you everywhere who love us and whom we love.

EXPLANATION

—Unless otherwise noted: all Scriptures are quoted from the New American Standard Bible. The Lockman Foundation — 1960, 1962, 1963, 1971, 1972, 1973, 1975, are used by permission.

—All quotations from the King James Version are identified as (KJ).

—All author's paraphrases or adaptations are identified as (JB).

—All quotations from the Amplified New Testament are identified as (AMP), and are also used by permission from the Lockman Foundation, c 1958.

—We don't know all there is to know about raising children yet, but we have a commission to share some of the basics of that which we have learned. If you have ideas that may improve this presentation, or, if you disagree, or wish to recommend any other books on the subject, please let us know, because we are still learning. Are you? May God Himself be making real to your own heart, that part which is also inspired of Him, within these pages.

—If you have suggestions, love offerings for the fulfillment of The Great Commission, or criticism, please feel free to write to us at:

Great Commission Ministries
P.O. 7123, Minneapolis,
MN., 55407

—We love you!!!

1

SELL YOUR CHILD???

"COME QUICK, I JUST RAN OVER DAWN JOY!" While we were pioneering and pastoring a metropolitan church near downtown Phoenix, I was ministering to some dear ones after an evening service, when one of the young deacons came bursting through the front door and yelled, "Come quick, I just ran over Dawn Joy!" Dawn Joy was our little three year old girl, prettiest little thing you ever did see, with sparkly blue eyes and soft long curly hair. When I did run outside, what I found was worse than what I had expected.

Her pretty head was cracked like an egg, from ear to ear. Her face looked like hamburger. Both ear drums were broken. She was blind in one eye. There were tire tracks on her back. Blood was streaming from her nose, mouth, and ears. Before we pulled out of the drive-way, the church members were on their faces in earnest prayer, (it was needed). And before we reached the hospital, other churches had received word, including the Katherine Kuhlman Foundation and the Oral Roberts prayer tower and they were praying, (it was needed).

The hospital we just "happened" to go to turned out to be the best neuro-surgical center in that part of the country and they were waiting for us when we arrived. The doctor became angry at me when I expressed concern for her eardrums. He said, "Man, we are trying to get her to live through the night, and you are worried about her ears!"

So I prayed. With an awful ache in my throat, and tears streaming down my face, I said, "Father, we dedicated Dawn Joy to You when she was just a new baby, so she's Your property, we are just the stewards. And since she is Your property, we give You permission to take her life if You want to, but of course we would prefer that You don't. Nevertheless, I promise You Lord that if You do take her, that we won't be bitter or resentful. I repent Lord for anything I may have been or done that may have directly or indirectly contributed to this accident, and give You permission to teach any of us anything through this that You want us to learn. And since Your Word says that we are to give You thanks in everything and for everything, I thank You, Lord God, Lord Jesus Christ, for this accident and I worship You in the midst of this circumstance."

While in the hospital, Dawn would sing through her head bandages when the nurses would come to change her dressing, songs she had learned like, "I Believe God!" and "The B-I-B-L-E, YES, That's the Book For Me" and "Jesus Loves Me!" and others. (We still have a tape recording of this.) But within only 9 days from the date of the accident, Dawn was

24

released from the hospital!!! The only problem remaining was that she was still blind in one eye. So, two weeks after the accident, Karen and Dawn Joy were told by the eye specialist, "We don't know if she will ever see out of that eye, but if she does, the earliest indication will be not before six months."

"BIG JOE"

But when Karen and Dawn left the doctor's office, they were met in the hallway by a tall "man" who laid his hand on Dawn Joy's head, and said, "She will see by next week at this time." Karen replied, "Praise the Lord, my husband and I are believing God for a real miracle!" She continued, "I'm Karen and this is Dawn Joy." The tall man said. "I'm Big Joe." Karen said, "May the Lord bless you!" and "Big Joe" said, "And may the Lord bless you." Then he walked away. One week later to the day, Dawn Joy spoke from out of the back seat of the car in which we were riding, "Look Mommie, I can see!!!!!" And so she could, and you can see by looking at her picture, or if you get to meet her in person, that she is perfectly healed, and beautiful with soft curly hair and sparkling blue eyes! Thank You Dear Lord Jesus, Father God, Creator King of all the Universe!!!!!!!

There is one special point that we would like to make at this point - and that is that Dawn Joy was definitely NOT our property, nor was she even our child any more because we had given her to Jesus Christ, to God. We had dedicated her to the Lord, and He had only LOANED her back to us, for us to raise for Him as mere stewards of her upbringing for Himself. And we are happy to report that Dawn Joy has come to agree with this commitment that we made, and has, of her own choice, yielded herself also completely to the Lord God of the Universe!

SELL YOUR CHILD?

Sell your child? Well, some of you may have the kind of children or circumstances that are so hideous, or perhaps you have such a low opinion of yourself or your child that you would be so tempted. But, our counsel to you is that instead of selling your child, that you lovingly trustingly GIVE your child or children away to the Lord Jesus Christ, Father God. Then eagerly volunteer to raise that child for the Lord, never for a moment forgetting Whose child it is or to Whom it belongs, giving accountability for the manner in which you raise that child for the Lord. And while you're at it, please be giving yourself away to Him as well. Look at this if you will, God will not force His way into any area of your life against your will. Love never intentionally intimidates, for where love exists, intentional intimidation does not, for they are mutually exclusive terms, that is, cannot exist together. How many men woo and win their wife with candy, sweet talk and flowers, but after the honeymoon, begin to intentionally intimidate while wondering where her love has gone. God does not intimidate, but always woos and lovingly draws us until He sees that we will or will not respond, and to what extent. There is a real sense in which God sends

26

no one to hell, but that all who go there do so of their own free choice, having been offered to come dwell in the palace of the King of the Universe. They end up in hell by default, because they neglected to accept the King's pardon! Please make sure! (For more information on Hell, please write and ask for our article we have written about Hell.)

THE KINGDOM OF GOD — YOUR HOME

The thing closest to the heart of God is the Kingdom of God. It is the thing the prophets spoke about, and was THE message of John the Baptist, of Jesus, of the early disciples, of the Apostle Paul and of the disciples of these days also. (For a more complete discussion on the Kingdom of God, please refer to the author's first book, *HOW TO RULE THE WORLD or SEEK 1st THE KINGDOM OF GOD.)* But for our purposes here, suffice it to say that THE KINGDOM OF GOD IS WHAT GOD IS THE KING OF.

In other words, if your life has Christ as its King, and you are living, loving, acting, parenting, spousing the way He wants, then your life is a beautiful picture of the Kingdom of God. So it is also with your home. If your family is born again and living, functioning the way Christ the Creator King of Everything wants, then your home is to that extent a beautiful demonstration in the practical realm of the Kingdom of God in the here and now.

HOW TO JOIN THE KINGDOM OF GOD

Jesus said, "With all the earnestness I possess I tell you this: Unless you are born again, you can never get

27

into the Kingdom of God." John 3, verse 3, (Living Bible). And the way to be born again is described in Revelation 3, verse 20 — (I'll put it in simple words), "Look! I have been standing at the door of your life and I am knocking. If you will open the door to your life and invite Me to come in, I will come in, and we will have wonderful fellowship together." But the door has no latch on the outside as Christ will not FORCE His way into any area of your life. You may pray this prayer:

"Dear Heavenly Father, I open wide the door of my life to You, and I Invite You, Lord Jesus Christ to come into My life and BE my Saviour, BE my Lord, BE my Life. I confess my sins to You and turn away from them. Be all that YOU are, in me, through me from now on, at all times, and in everything, take over completely, and fill me to overflowing with Your Love, Your Holy Spirit, Your Peace, Your cleansing, healing, forgiving Power, Your Life, All that You are in me, through me. In Jesus' Name. Amen."

A MAN'S HOME IS WHO'S CASTLE
or
DON'T OWN YOUR OWN HOME

In Matthew 7, verse 21, Jesus said something interesting. (Doesn't He always!) He says, "Not every one that saith unto Me, 'Lord', 'Lord', shall enter into the Kingdom Of Heaven; but that DOETH the will of My Father which is in heaven."

In Luke 14, verses 25 to 34, Jesus tells us clearly that it is necessary, absolutely — to absolutely give

ALL to Him, especially our own life, OR we simply will NOT be His disciples. But look at what we receive in return! We simply exchange all that we are for all that He is, exchange all that we have for all that He has! In almost exactly the same way that you don't particularly care about what happens to someone elses' property, Jesus will not assume responsibility for what has not been given to Him. He will not violate your will. He assumes partial responsibility for that which has been only partially committed to Him. And Christ assumes total and full and complete responsibility for the Life and lives and families and homes that are totally dedicated and surrendered and yielded to Him!!! Your child now belongs to God!!

SIGN THE BLANK CONTRACT!

One thing I learned during my years as a real estate agent, and as a probation officer: "Never sign a blank contract." But there's something that I've learned in my walk with God. He lovingly insists on it! In the Living Bible, He says in John 7:17, "If any of you really determines to do God's will, then you will certainly know whether My teaching is from God or is merely My own." So many times people have said, "Lord Jesus, You show me what Your will, plan, or purpose is for my life, then I'll tell You whether I approve." But God doesn't deal with folks who feel like this.

No, Dear One, God has your best interest in mind and asks that you take courage, and sign the blank contract. He'll fill in the terms and conditions later.

REVIEW QUESTIONS - CHAPTER 1

1. What do we mean, "Our kids are not ours?"

2. When God commands us to give thanks "IN" and "FOR" everything, does He really mean that?

3. Who do you think "Big Joe" is?

4. Why are the words "love" and "intimidation", mutually   exclusive terms?

5. Tell briefly how to be born again.

6. What do we mean, "Don't own your own home?"

7. What do we mean, "Sign the blank contract!"?

8. Make a list, in order of importance, the things in your life that you consider important.

2

FIRST THINGS FIRST
PRIORITIES
WHAT'S MOST IMPORTANT

A. YOU KNOW WHO

Please consider God's formula for having a perfect family. If we don't follow His blueprint, we can't blame the mess on Him. So here are some principles that can make all of the difference.

Look at this: Jesus says in Matthew 6, verse 33, "But seek ye first the Kingdom of God, and His righteousness; and all these things shall be added unto you." And in another place, Psalm 37, "Delight yourself in the Lord, and He will give you the desires of your heart." These Scriptures indicate that if we put God at the top of the priority list, that He will make everything else be good for us, and will take care of everything else. One the other hand, if we don't have Him as head of everything, then we are back to that attitude, "I'm smarter than God." Without Him in control, they better hope their "good luck" holds out, cause they're gonna need it! But there is a next priority that you will enjoy.

SUPER PRIORITY - YOU!!!

Remember the Scripture that says, "Love your neighbor as yourself"? But how can you love your neighbor unless you love yourself? Or how can you minister life to others unless you feel good about yourself? The very next chapter explains how you can have a fabulous self image that will really be a gift to you from the Lord! Suffice it to say here that God really does consider you to be very very important, and that He really does have your best interest in mind. You are so very very important to Him.

YOUR SPOUSE

Your spouse comes next, and ahead of the children, the house or the dog. Because unless you put your spouse first, you may end up not having a spouse, a house or the children; you may keep the dog. We really recommend the book to you by this author on marriage called, *THE SEXUAL MINISTRY.* (The book deals with far more than sex.)

THE CHILDREN

This priority is what this book is all about, so we will let the rest of the book speak for the children.

THE OUTLAWS

Who comes next, after your children? Your family!!! But what family? Several times the Gospels describe when people told Christ that His brothers, sisters and mother were there to see Him. Whereupon Jesus replies, "Who is my mother, brother or sister?"

And then pointing to His disciples, He said, "The person who does the will of My Father in heaven, is My mother, My sister, and My brother." And these are YOUR mother, brother and sister also, if you are totally committed to Christ as your Lord and Master. One of the greatest principles to learn is that we are to constantly relate to people on God's terms, and not on ours or theirs.

THE POSSESSIONS

Story is told of a farmer had two cows, and told his wife he was going to give one of them to the Lord. "Which one, the brown, or the white one?" the wife asked. "Haven't made up my mind yet" came his reply. That night the brown one died. When the husband found out about it next day, he announced to his wife, "Well, it looks like God's cow died." Funny ain't it? Bible says we are to honor God with our tithes, (one/tenth), the first fruits, not the last leftovers. Another story, I think it's true, tells of some missionaries got a package from home which included this note, "Tea bags — Only been used once." That's the way some people's lives are — left overs after they wasted most of it on something else. (I suppose that's better than nothing, eh?) How often we drop off to sleep, without having spent quality time before the Lord in His Word or in prayer.

We once again would like to respectfully refer you to the book, *How To Rule The World, or Seek lst the Kingdom Of God,* especially the chapter entitled, "$$". The book deals with Life's priorities. In this

33

chapter on "$$", we talk about a newspaper advertisement that was begging for money because they wanted to rescue dogs from being eaten in Asia. The contributions are even "tax exempt"! Yet we know of people who will burn in hell forever, because Christians and others would rather spend or invest their money in things less important. For example, the country of China is open right now for the first time in three decades to receive Bibles at a cost of less than $1 each. Millions of them would give their very life to see it happen.

Many of us would rather buy dog food. (By the way, any money sent to us earmarked for Bibles, (not dog food), will be forwarded to them, and your contributions to supply Bibles, or for us to otherwise fulfill the Great Commission, are "tax deductible"! Make your checks out to "The Kingdom of God", and send them to Great Commission Ministries, P.O. 7123, Minneapolis, MN., 55407.)

THE DOG(S)

We have a lady friend of the family, who has told us in the past that her dogs were all she had to live for, and that if they died or were taken away, that she would commit suicide. Sounds like her life might have gone to the dogs, eh? Another lady actually struggled between staying with the will of God and staying with her dog. The poor girl had got turned around on dog, spelled it backwards, and had come up with a g-o-d. The Word of the Lord to her, and to all, was, (and is), "Thy dog is a dog." Reminds me of those drivers who, when a dog or kitty cat runs out in front of them, they will rather drive into a tree or crash the car with themselves, their kids or YOU, rather than hit the darling doggie. Ought to ask the driver that question next time before you auto. Ask the driver that ques... never mind.

REVIEW QUESTIONS - CHAPTER 2

1. Whose smarter, you, or God?

2. List 2 Scriptures that deal with priorities.

3. Who did Jesus say that His brother, sister and mother were?

4. List, in order of importance the priority list as it should read.

5. How much money are you willing to give to see Bibles placed in the hands of the Chinese people at less than $1.00 each?

6. What do we mean, "Some people have their dog spelled backwards"? Do you?

3

HOW TO WHAT WHO'S
WHEN AND WHY

Please allow me to ask a silly question. "WHO'S
SMARTER, YOU OR GOD?" (forgive me for
mentioning God so early in the book, but I just
couldn't hold off any longer.) The reason why we
asked this question is that some folks actually act like
they think they are smarter than God! They seem to
say, "I can run my life better than God can. I can
decide for me more wisely than He. I'll decide for
myself who I'm to marry, what school to attend, what
career to choose, without consulting God." And this
idea carries over to this matter of raising the children.
Why is it that we will contrive to do it practically any
way but God's way? "If all else fails, I'll ask Dr.
Shock." (Something like "Why pray, when you can
worry!")

But we would like to make a loving suggestion.
That you read through your Bible ALL THE WAY
without skipping any parts, starting with Matthew 1.
Begin today, and as soon as you finish each chapter,
be sure and write the day's date down at the end of
each chapter you read. This way you will not forget

how far you have read. Don't skip any parts and don't worry about understanding. And as you go through the Bible, pay special attention to what God has to show you about the family. In our statistics that we have been accumulating from the seminars that we have conducted, and the places we have ministered in the United States and Brazil, we believe that less than 1 out of every 100 born again believers in Christ has ever read the entire Bible through without skipping any parts. While in other countries people are risking and giving their lives for even small portions of the Bible. This ministry is involved with helping get Bibles into the hands of such as these if you are interested also in helping.

How long do you think it would take to read the Bible through? Or just the New Testament? I sat down with the children the other day with a calculator and a stop watch and read aloud two pages of the Scriptures at an 'average' speed. Then, we multiplied times the number of pages in the New Testament and came up with only twelve hours and for the entire Bible, approximately fifty!!! Computer geniuses I know have told me that it is still impossible to get from a computer what has not been programmed into it. God has promised that He will bring to our remembrance Scripture we have read, but there are no promises that He'll help us remember what we never 'remembranced'. So we are recommending that you start TODAY, and while reading it through, make special note of every reference to the family by marking a symbol in the margin pertaining to it.

But to return to the question: if God is smarter than you, (He is), and has your best interest in mind, (He does), then it is only logical and right to let Him guide in the decision making process, in your fulfillment of His fabulous destiny for your life!!! Can you see the importance of this?

GOD'S RECIPE

With this business of raising children, we often fail to get God's results because we fail to follow God's formula. There is just one verse from the Scriptures that we will refer to here. It is found in Titus 2:4 and indicates that the mature women are to teach the less mature women how "To love their husbands, to love (and raise) their children." The picture comes to mind of a little old woman pinching a younger woman's rosy cheek and wagging her bony finger at her and saying, "Now dearie, love your husband and be good to your children." But that's NOT what the Scriptures had in mind for an instructor. Yet in our society, we somehow expect and demand that the woman intuitively know it all, by simply saying, "I do" at the altar without TRAINING her HOW to "do" at home. Then we wonder why they didn't live 'happily ever after'! This is the reason for the need of books and seminars and trained counsellors like those mentioned above which definitely DO help to enable the dear ones to live happily ever after! Now, these books and seminars are available in your area, helping to bring forth wise counsel to you from the Lord, and then from the Lord Jesus in you to many dear ones.

REVIEW QUESTIONS - CHAPTER 3

1. Who is smarter, you or God?

2. Have you ever read through the entire Bible without skipping any parts?

3. Are you willing to start today, (if you are not already doing so)?

4. Approximately how long would it take the average reader to read through the New Testament without skipping any parts if he wouldn't have to stop? The entire Bible?

5. What is God's recipe for women to know how to love her husband and raise her children?

6. Have you read the book, *How To Rule The World, or Seek 1st The Kingdom Of God?*

7. Have you read our book, *The Sexual Ministry?*

4

THE KING'S GREATEST SECRET
or
HOW TO BE PERFECT

If someone could give to you a perfect formula that would make you into a "perfect parent", would you be interested??? Believe it or not, there are many parents that would NOT be interested! But here, in this chapter, we will present to you a simple, easy to follow formula, that God guarantees will show you **HOW TO BE A PERFECT PARENT!!!!!!!**

THE KING'S GREATEST SECRET ! ! !

God has a Secret!!! He would like to tell it to You! The angels and men of God wanted to know this Secret, but God wouldn't tell them for thousands of years. Then God told The Secret to the Church through the Apostle Paul and the other apostles and prophets. That Secret was lost and forgotten again during the dark ages, but now is being told again in this special time to the Church. It's the King's Greatest Secret! It needs to be told so very much. Almost no one in the Church today knows The Secret.

41

We have ministered in many churches across the country and in most of them we ask a certain question to find out if they know The Secret. And in none of the places where we have ministered have they known. The question we asked them was, "What did Jesus take of ours with Him to the cross?" Will you take a minute to answer this before you continue?

We get answers, all of them correct but not complete, like "He took our sins, our sicknesses, our worries, burdens, fears etc." We say, "That's true that He took these so we can be forgiven, healthy, and without worry (some folks cast their burdens upon Yahweh, the Mighty Right NOW God, but as a fisherman casts, they sit and reel these burdens back to themselves.) But the people still have not told the main thing Christ took with Him to the cross! I suppose the reason they do not know, is that it requires a revelation of God, or one who has a revelation from God, to share The Secret, before they can know. What a Wonderful Mystery!

MOUNT PO-PO-KAT-A-MA-TEL or, "THE LONG DISTANCE GOD"

We believe that more than 9,999 Christians out of 10,000 relate to God in one of the following incorrect ways:

They relate to God "long distance". That is, they visualize God as living way out beyond Mount Popokatamatel somewhere, and that if they pray real long and loud and hard, that maybe God will hear them, and that maybe, but less likely, the answer will get back. The song says that Jesus leans out over the battlements of heaven, and yells down the distance, "'Hold the fort, for I am coming', Jesus signals still. Wave the answer back to heaven, 'By Thy grace we will.'"

The other incorrect (We shall see in a moment why these are incorrect), concept of God is that of "A little bitty God inside of a BIG person with still BIGGER problems". We invite Jesus to come into our hearts, and so He does, not as our very LIFE, in most cases, but as a sometimes thought of "Guest". (I don't like, nor will I say that prayer, "Come, Lord Jesus, be our guessed...") I don't want Him to be a guest, I want Him to come in as the Master, my very LIFE!!! But some of us, when we pray to Jesus hiding way down deep in our hearts somewhere, we get our own echoes back as if we were talking into a well. God wants to be very Very VERY much more real to us than these.

THE SECRET!!!

The Secret is found in plain sight in a multitude of places in the Bible, especially in places like John 17, Ephesians, Romans, Galatians, Colossians, etc. BEWARE that when you hear this Secret, that you not think too lightly or casually. The proof that you got the Secret will be that you will be able to consistently keep your heart and attitude and spirit right. In fact, if you REALLY get the Secret, as the following Scriptures indicate, there will be no difference between who Christ is at the Father's right hand, and who He is - - - in you!

43

The Secret Mystery is this: When Christ went to the cross, He took US with Him there! When He died, WE died! When He was buried, WE were buried with ALL of our insufficiencies, inadequacies, inferiorities, insecurities, inabilities, and instabilities!!!! Everything negative, nasty, weak, or sinful about us, He took to the cross because He took US to the cross. Oh, dear one, if you grasp hold of this Secret it will make all the difference in the world for you! It will mean the difference between Christ living your life, and you living your life; between you trying to speak good things, and Christ speaking His words through you!

Lord Jesus, please make this plain and understandable. We believe together that You will make the Mystery clear. "I praise Thee, O Father, Lord of heaven and earth, that Thou didst hide these things from the wise and intelligent, and didst reveal them to babes. Yes, Father for thus it was well pleasing in Thy sight" Matt. 11:25 and Luke 10:21.

Please let me tell you more about The Secret. When The Lord Jesus Christ went to the cross, He took you with Him there! YOU WERE THERE when they crucified my Lord! Christ looked ahead in time and saw you and decided that He could not help you any other way, that He could not beat or bless you into being what He wants you to be, could not educate or "religious" you adequately, but that the only hope for you was to take you with Him to the Cross and kill you dead, along with all of your negative nature and qualities, and bury you. Unlike many self-help books, Christ does not try to get you to "hype" or hypnotize,

con or convince yourself into thinking that you are really good or nice, adequate or o.k., but that you are horribly hopeless and hideously helpless, apart from Christ taking you to the cross with Him and putting all of your self to death and burying it in the tomb with Him. So you do not need to kill yourself or commit suicide, nor do your friends, because Jesus Christ lovingly killed us softly already. But that is not the end of the story!

WOW! YOU REALLY ARE
SOMETHING AFTER ALL!!!

When Christ rose from the tomb HE RAISED US UP as a whole, new, beautiful, wonderful, adequate, sufficient, glorious, superior, perfect, able, stable, secure creation in His image in newness of Life so He could come into us and BE our Life, Live our Life, BE our perfection, BE our righteousness!!!

Perhaps you would like to see this Secret in the Scriptures. The following Verses can become attainable in the practical realm of the nitty gritty now:

I Cor. 15:57	Victory
II Cor. 2:14-16	Victory always everywhere
Rom. 6:7,18,22	Free from sin
Col. 3:1-3	Risen with Christ our life
Eph. 2:6	Seated in Christ
Ps. 16:11	Fullness of joy; joy unspeakable

46

Ps.91	Secret Place of the Most High
Eph. 1:3,4	Every blessing
Ne. 8:10	Joy of the Lord strength
I Cor. 2:16	Mind of Christ
Ph. 4:13	Can do all things through Christ
Jude 24	Walk blamelessly
Matt. 28:18	All power and authority
Matt. 5:14	We are the light of the World
Ph. 1:21	To Live Is Christ
II Cor. 9:8	All power and authority
John 14:13	What ever we ask
John 10:10	Abundant Life
II Pet. 1:1-4	We have all things for life
Rom. 8:37	More than conquerors
I John 4:17	We are as He is
Matt. 19:26	All things are possible
I John 2:6	We can know the mysteries of the Kingdom of God
Col. 1:25-29	Mystery of the gospel of the ages
I Cor. 1:30	Christ is made unto us wisdom, righteousness, sanctification and redemption.

Galatians 2:20 says, "I have been crucified with Christ, and it is no longer I who live, BUT CHRIST LIVES IN ME!!!" In Colossians, God says that CHRIST IS OUR LIFE! The Bible says, "For me to

47

live IS Christ" (Phil. 1:21), and "We HAVE the mind of Christ" (I Cor. 2:16), and "As He [Christ] is SO ARE WE IN THIS WORLD" I John 4:17. Oh, dear heart, I pray for you with deep, unutterable longing and faith "That the God of our Lord Jesus Christ, the Father of Glory, may give you a spirit of wisdom and of revelation in the knowledge of Him! I pray that the eyes of your heart may be enlightened so that you may KNOW..." (Eph. 1:17,18.)

THE ROAD TO HELL IS PAVED WITH GOOD EXCUSES

Do you realize that if God Himself stepped down from a fluffy white cloud and offered an easy way for us to be perfect, that many Christians would simply not be interested?! The "Good News" message, (that we can walk before the Lord pleasing in motive, thought, word and deed), would be, to many "Christians", very "bad news". A major reason is that they want an excuse for their sinning! Another reason is that they would have to change their "doctrine" and when it comes to doctrine, some folks would rather go to hell than switch!

I have gone from door to door trying to persuade people to invite Jesus Christ into their hearts as their Lord, as a necessary FIRST step in escaping the eternal flames of hell, but instead they most OFTEN answer, "Look, I've got my own —-. I was born a ——-, I was raised a ——-, and I'm going to die a ——-!" Most of them might as well have added, "And I'm going to go to hell a ——!" Church membership

48

does NOT give a person entrance into the Kingdom of God but only by being born again, as Jesus declares in John 3:3-5, and Revelation 3:20, where He tells us how. "I'm standing at the door of your life and I'm knocking. If you will invite Me to come in to your life and heart as Saviour King of everything, then I will come in." That's how to be born again!

But after we're born again it's VERY important that we don't begin making excuses for not measuring up to God's will for us, because contrary to what we may have been taught, there is no excuse for not doing the will of God! I've often wondered what would have happened in the Garden of Eden if Adam would not have tried to make excuses, when God came and asked him why he "messed up". Instead, Adam said, "The woman!" (Then he added), "Whom YOU GAVE to me..." I wonder what would have happened if Adam would have said, "Lord, please don't blame Eve. Let all the blame be upon me. She's the weaker vessel, and I should have been looking out for her. Or what if Eve would have said the same. Instead she blamed the serpent. The only good thing I can think of to say about the devil is that when God came to him, he didn't pass the buck, or blame. Never mind the fact that he didn't have any place to pass it!

But it is impossible for us to be EXCUSING and REPENTING at the same time. Besides, God will NOT forgive what we are excusing. Most Christians have been brainwashed, hypnotized or otherwise programmed into thinking that "nobody's perfect". They even use this kind of reasoning as an excuse for

49

sinning in the first place and for not repenting in the second place. The excuse, "I'm only human after all,..." is typical, but definitely counterproductive. Remember, the Lord gives in the Word, many victory promises: I Corinthians 10:13 says that, "There has NO temptation taken you but such as is common to man: but GOD IS FAITHFUL, who will NOT let you be tempted above what you are able, but will with the temptation also make a way to escape that you may be able to bear it." And in II Corinthians 2:14, "Now thanks be unto God, who ALWAYS causes us to TRIUMPH IN CHRIST, and makes manifest the savour of His knowledge by us in every place." (Victory=Always-everywhere!!!) And Romans 8:37,—"...In ALL THESE THINGS WE ARE MORE THAN CONQUERORS THROUGH HIM that loved(s) us!" And, Philippians 4:13, "I can do ALL things through Christ who strengthens me!!!"

A QUICK BUT PERHAPS NECESSARY LOOK AT A WRONG DOCTRINE

Intricately interwoven into the fabric of our thinking is some wrong doctrine that has been "bee-ing" spuriously spread throughout nearly all of Christendom. Protestants and Catholics, every demonination - it seems that hardly anyone has been spared. This doctrine of the dualism of nature, concerns our attitude toward our bodies, toward pleasure, our flesh, perfection, victory, - towards Life itself. A fresh revelation realization of The King's Greatest Secret changes all this.

50

MONSTROUS MANICHEAN MADNESS

The Church was fully free of faulty thinking in this area until about the fourth and fifth century after Christ, when a funny but phoney philosophy of "dualism" infiltrated the Church from a man called "the father of Christian philosophy and theology". He introduced a warped way of thinking into the Church that was not corrected by the theologians or philosophers that were to follow. Here is the man, the doctrine and the correction to his approach.

St Augustine, 354-430 A.D. was a Greek Manicheist philosopher prior to his coming into the Church. Here, we quote from the World Book Dictionary, "Manichean (man' e ke" en), a member of a Gnostic sect, arising in Persia in the 200's A.D., compounded of Christian, Buddhistic, Zoroastrian, and other beliefs, and maintaining a theological dualism in which the body and matter were identified with darkness and evil, and the soul, striving to liberate itself, was identified with light and goodness." In other words, while the Hebrews believed matter and the body to be bad or good, depending upon the use to which it was put, - the Manichiests believed, and taught that the body was evil, and that every thing that the body did, or was, or said, was only always exceedingly sinful. Sound familiar? Nearly every church and catechism and liturgy we know of has something of this within it. Some have even given the illustration that inside every person there is a white dog nature and a black dog nature and that the one that wins is the one you say "sic 'em" to (or feed) the most. That's what we mean by "dualism".

The Hebrews said that matter, a pen, a human body was not bad in itself, but that its goodness or badness was determined by what one did with that matter or pen or human body. This is why, in Romans, Paul says that "the instruments of our body are slaves of righteousness if we yield them to do righteous things, and that they are instruments of unrighteousness if we yield them to do unrighteous things."

But the manicheans said that our body members are bad, because they were made of substance, of material, of matter. So in Augustine's writings, he says that it is a sin to watch a dog chase a rabbit. Why? Because the body gets excited and involved, and says, "Let's see now, is the dog going to catch the rabbit, or is the rabbit going to catch the dog!" Augustine said, "I have learned to take my food as medicine." In other words, he disciplined himself to the place that a big juicy piece of beefsteak tasted like cod liver oil, just so his body would not get all involved, excited, and sinful. My well rounded mother told me one time that every act of sex was sinful. (She had four grown children!) She quoted David's verse, "I was born and conceived in sin." She didn't know the Jewish tradition about David's personal family situation. I said, "Mother, what a terrible thing to say about us kids." (We discuss this more fully in our book, *THE SEXUAL MINISTRY*, available at Great Commission Ministries, P.O. 7123, Mpls., MN., 55407. Love

52

Offerings, to help provide for this and other books and Bibles for others, are tax deductible.)

The real question is NOT "Can I keep from sinning?" but "Is God great enough to keep me from sinning?!." Is He? If someone asks me, "Do you ever get a wrong spirit or attitude toward your wife or children or anyone?" or if they say, "Don't you ever sin?" I respond, "I don't recommend it!" or "We're not in favor of it." If they argue, "Do you actually think a person can get through the day without sinning!?" I respond, "We'd advise it."

Mark Twain allegedly wrote in his memoirs, "Went to church today. Preacher preached on sin. Only problem was, I couldn't rahtly tell whether he was for it, 'r agin' it!" You know? Sometimes a body cain't tell by looking at some Christians' lives and doctrines whether or not they're in favor of sin or against it either!!!

HOW LONG CAN YOU LIVE
WITHOUT SINNING?

I John 1:9 says that "If we confess our sins, God is faithful and just, ...and will cleanse us from - (not much, or most, but) - ALL unrighteousness!!!" Let's say you just "I John 1:9'ed" it. How much unrighteousness do you got left in yuh? Doesn't it say cleansed from ALL?!. How long can you stay cleansed from all unrighteousness through the power of God, and by the Strength, and through the Life of God lived through you??? 5 seconds? 5 minutes, by God your Strength? 5 hours, through Christ, your

Power? 5 days, with Christ as your Life? 5 decades, with Jesus Christ AS YOUR RIGHTEOUSNESS!!!!!?!. (Please refer to the above list of Scriptures here. Or would you rather continue on in your excuse making and cannibalizing?)

IF GOD DIDN'T MAKE LITTLE GREEN APPLES IN MINNEAPOLIS

Paul, in Philippians 3, uses the word 'perfect' in two different ways. In verse 12 he says he's not perfect and in verse 15 he says that he IS!!! (I wonder why we only always hear that he's not?) Imagine, if you will, a little green apple, just barely past the blossom stage, a little bitty nubbin of a thing. But it's perfect! No worms, germs, dust, crust, must or rust. It's not dashed, bashed, crashed, hashed or gnashed. And now, can you picture a perfectly perfect apple that's ruby, rudy, rosy, red, ripe and juicy? If it were any more ripe, it would be rotten; and if it were any less ripe it would be sour and woody. Please ask yourself this question: What particular things are necessary for a smaller apple's growth and development into this mature apple? Are bruises, or worms or rot necessary? Is "hanging in there" necessary? — To endure the long cold nights? the hot summer days, the wind, and rain?

Some folks seem to think that rebellion, back-slidings, detours, lapses, wrong attitudes and spastic silliness are all necessary to our growth and development in God.

There is a discipline, but it is a discipline that pertains to the new person or man in Christ Jesus, and

54

not the old man or old self or nature. The old life HAS BEEN crucified with Christ - not "is being". We don't believe in beating the dead carcass. That would be wasted effort, and futile.

So, we see that the flesh is neither good nor bad in or of itself, but depending upon the use to which it is put. Adam, before he fell, had flesh, and our redeemed bodies will be flesh, even Jesus had flesh. Hebrews 5 speaks of Jesus, "Who in the days of His flesh...offered up prayers with strong crying and tears...and...though He were a Son, yet learned He obedience through the things which He suffered. And being made perfect, He became the Author of eternal salvation unto all them that obey Him." Wasn't Jesus already perfect? Of course! But here we see that He also needed to "become perfect". Can we be perfect in the I John 1:9 "cleansed from ALL unrighteousness" sense? Of course, but we also need to become perfect in the "ripe apple" sense of "growing in grace and in the knowledge of the Son of God" and in the sense of Paul's pressing "toward the mark for the prize of the high calling of God in Christ Jesus" - the fulfillment of our adventures and destinies and callings of God!!!

CRISIS AND PROCESS

So there is both a crisis and a process to every experience that we are to have in God: the new birth, the Lordship of Christ, Sanctification, (dedicated and made holy), the Holy Spirit, etc.

Ask some "Christians" if they are saved, and they'll say, "I dunno, I'm workin' on it." (The Bible says we can KNOW! I Jn.5). But because they are always working on the process of salvation, without the crisis of having been born again, they won't be...., because they are always GOING THROUGH the door, but never quite get IN. But then you ask others if they're saved, and they say, "Ya sure, I got saved 90 years ago!" But too many of them got saved and stuck! They got through the door and then went to sleep for 89 years. The same thing is true of the Holy Spirit. Some believe only in the process of being filled while others got "it", and got stuck, (or sprung leaks!). And the same thing is true with The King's Greatest Secret - BOTH the crisis of appropriation AND the process of abiding in Him — moment by moment; both are necessary.

ARE YOU NOW READY TO DIE - THEN LIVE!!!

You simply: # 1. Know and "RECKON YOURSELF TO HAVE BEEN CRUCIFIED WITH CHRIST" (Rom. 6:6 - this is the crises), and # 2. THEN CONSIDER AND RECKON YOURSELF (here is the process) AS "DEAD INDEED UNTO SIN, SELF AND satan, but alive unto God through Jesus Christ our Lord!!! (Rom.6:11) ALLELU-JAHWEH!!! Thank you, Dear Lord Jesus, for taking us to the cross with You and for raising us up with You in newness of Life in You. Lord God, we receive You to be all that You are, in us, now and forever more. Amen. Jesus said, "BE YE THEREFORE PERFECT, EVEN AS YOUR FATHER IN HEAVEN IS PERFECT." Matt. 5:48. Jesus, as always, meant just what He said! He meant "BE as perfect as God!" Or would you prostitute and change and twist and warp and non-effectualize the Word of God here or any other place?

It does NOT mean "try to be perfect" nor "be perfect sometime after your body has rotted", nor "give up on being perfect", nor "it's impossible to be perfect", nor "wish that you were perfect", nor "God isn't great enough to make or keep me perfect", nor "be theoretically perfect", nor any of that kind of silliness. 'Would be' disciples of the Kingdom, WON'T BE disciples of the Kingdom of God as long as they are messing with the commands of the King of God's Kingdom in this way! One who changes the commands of the King is a Kingdom anarchist and traitor. When someone asks, "What does this Verse mean?" the best answer is, "The Bible means what it says!" because the King means what He says. I believe that whenever there is a disagreement about a Scripture, it is because one or more of them is not willing to accept what the Scripture and King says.

THE GREATEST MOMENT OF MY LIFE

One day Patty Troug at Bethel College told me, "John, as long as you are calling 'idealistic', 'unattainable', or 'theoretical' what God calls necessary, practical, available, and attainable, YOU are calling God a LIAR!!! I had thrown a book away from me in disgust, *FOREVER TRIUMPHANT*, by Huegel, in which he quoted II Corinthians 2:14, "Thanks be unto God who in Christ ALWAYS causes

57

us to triumph and manifests Christ through us in EVERY place!" (JB) Victory, at ALL times and in every place! I had said "that's too idealistic", but then I realized, as a result of Patricia's gentle rebuke, that I had been calling God a liar in that He had said, "Victory always and everywhere." And I had said, "Impossible". I did not want to call God a liar anymore, so I went to my room, got out my Bibles, KJV, AMP, Gdspd, Greek N.T., etc., and laid them out on Bruce Leafblad's vacant bunk, and got down on my knees in order to see just what God DID say. Sure enough, God said, "Perfect victory always" and "More than conquerors" and "Abundant Life" and "Joy unspeakable" and "Full of Glory" and "WE have the Mind of Christ" and "Christ our Life" and "whatever we ask" and "Greater works than these shall ye do" and "I can do all things through Christ" and "With God all things are possible" etc., etc., etc., etc. All these Bibles said the same thing, so I decided to do three things:

1. Confess every known sin, including having called God a liar;

2. Yield COMPLETELY to the Lord Jesus Christ. I told the Lord Jesus that I would be willing to be sick, maimed, killed, single, celibate, persecuted, misunderstood, forgotten, married to anyone He said (I was sure He was going to make me marry somebody really terrible). Anyway, I really meant business.

Now, these first two steps I had taken many times before, but I took them again. In fact, we should always keep up to date with the Lord, staying free from sin and staying in a totally yielded state.

3. Appropriate by faith the highest level walk in God's Spirit, with Christ AS our Life! Invite Jesus Christ come in to your life and take over completely as Saviour, Lord and Life!!!

Charles Trumble, in *The Life That Wins*, says that on this third step of faith, everything now depends. He suggested that we take a step of faith with total disregard for the presence (or lack of), accompanying signs or proofs, because the transaction must be based on faith rather than some feeling or tingle, etc. So, I remember reaching out my hand to the Lord God and saying, "Lord Jesus, I believe You have a walk for me that I haven't been experiencing; a relationship and an experience with You that I haven't had before. Lord Jesus, I don't know what to call it, and I don't know how to get it, but whatever You call it and however one gets it, I receive it from You now in cold, blind faith, not depending on outward feelings or 'signs' as the proof of the transaction. Thank You very much. In Jesus' Name, Amen."

Can you guess what happened? You guessed it. Nothing. Outwardly, or on a feeling level, that is. I felt really dead. Oh, I had accepted the Lord Jesus as my personal Saviour many years before, and I had yielded my Life to Him many times before. But the same thing had happened to me as would have happened in the Old Testament if one would have taken a clean lamb of the flock without blemish and then sacrificed the lamb under the hot Israel sun...and that's all. Can you imagine the mess? The sacrifice NEEDED the fire of God to come from heaven to light upon and consume the sacrifice as a sign of acceptance and anointing. But I rose from my knees there at Gerald Healy's house where Bruce Leafblad and I were roommates while attending Bethel College, November 1960, my senior year. I put away all my Bibles and climbed wearily into my top bunk. After I was settled down, I thought, "If anybody asked me to praise the Lord right now, it would be like someone asking me to praise a haystack." I suppose I was remembering a time when I had gone to visit a church and had tried to get "ba'tahzd wi' d' HoliGoz'" and the pastor was on one side telling me to say "Pah-rayz Gawd" just as loud as I could, whilst the preacher's wife was on the other side, encouraging me to say, "How'lay-lew'yuh" just as fast as I could. I recall how terribly difficult it had been to say either one either way. Folks who know me now are surprised that I didn't bound out of my mother's womb shouting "How'lay-lew'ya". One time, at Bible School, a staff member said the reason John Bohlen praised the Lord was because he had a 'sanguine' personality. I told her, "Yes, Joyce, the 47th Psalm says, 'O clap your hands, [all ye SANGUINES], shout unto God with the voice of triumph'!!!" By the way, that's not quite how it reads—it reads 'ALL YE PEOPLE'. So it's not just those with an enthusiastic personality that are to beautifully and enthusiastically and constantly worship the Lord: ALL of us are.

CATACLYSMIC REVOLUTION

Anyway, no sooner had that thought crossed my mind about praising a haystack, (indicating the lacking emotional level of positive feeling) when Christ BECAME my Life!, and I have never been the same since! It seemed like a great dam broke on the inside and there came explosively gushing over me, and through me, and to me, and from me, and upon me, and around me, from deep within and from high above the Glory of God, and the Joy of God, and the Love of God, and the Spirit of God, and the LIFE of God, and the Peace of God, and the Presence of God, and the Strength of God, and the Anointing of God, and the Overflowing, Effervescent Flooding Fullness of the Living God!!! I have never been the same! Fabulous! Incredible! Joyful! Invigorating! Beautiful! Astounding! Healing! Wonderful! Marvelous! Lasting! Satis-fying! Miraculous! Life-changing! Christ BECAME my Life! I saw myself as having been crucified with Christ, dead and buried with Christ, RISEN AND REIGNING WITH CHRIST JESUS in newness of Life, and seated IN Christ AT the Father's right hand, far over and above EVERYTHING that is named in heaven and on earth, and GLORIFIED IN HIM - Jesus Christ! This is described in Eph. 2, and Col. 3, Rom. 6, and Rom. 8, Eph. 3, II Cor. 3, etc., etc., etc. (Time out - for a Glory Spell and a happy dance!)

From the Amplified Bible, Eph. 3:19b - "That you may be filled (through all your being) unto all the fullness of God - [that is], may have the RICHEST measure of the Divine presence, and become a body WHOLLY filled and flooded with God Himself."

The question for all of us, no matter what our theological back-ground is: Are you FILLED WITH GOD RIGHT NOW? Jesus said, "He that believes in Me, out of his innermost being shall gush forth flooding torrents of Living Water continuously." Talkin' 'bout you?

Question - Are you full of God and His Holy Spirit right this moment? Are you up to date with Him and on excellent terms with Him right now? Do you minister and share from the overflow, or are you like a "small handful of water in a big empty barrel."

Pray with me?....

Dear Father God, thank You for providing unlimited anointing and every blessing, and having "given us all things that pertain to life and godliness". I ask You to BE my life; be ALL that You ARE, in me from now on. I reckon and consider my old life to be dead. I receive You as my "Wisdom, Righteousness, Sanctification, and Redemption". Be my Perfection, Love through me, speak Your Words Through me, pray through me. Thank You, Mighty-Right-Now God. I believe from now on I can do ALL things through Christ my Life, and that nothing shall be impossible IN YOU. In Jesus' Name, Amen.

There is a true story of a little boy who was looking intently into the baptistry after the baptism service, when his mother came up and asked him what he was doing. He said, "I'm looking for that 'old man' the pastor said we left in the water!" You see, this is the true meaning of baptism by immersion - our total identification with Christ in His crucifixion, death, burial, resurrection, ascension and glorification.

THE THIRD COMING OF CHRIST?!?!!.

Assume with me for a moment that God wants to return to the earth in a THIRD way. He came as a Babe, and He's coming in the clouds. But pretend with me, that between His 1st and 2nd Coming, He wants to come in a 3rd way. Imagine that this time, He wants to come disguised as a regular person, and that He wants to do it like this. Suppose someone is sitting in church, and has a cardiac attack, and dies, God forbid. Instead of rushing to give the person artificial rescuperation, the rest of the people, if they notice at all, think that that person just fell asleep for a minute. Suppose that before anyone else knows of this, Christ comes in to this person, blinks open his eyes, and starts walking around in his shoes in disguise, incognito, speaking, talking, loving, LIVING, His LIFE, - - - the very LIFE of Christ Himself!

He wants to be glorified and magnified now IN all who believe!! "When He shall come to be glorified IN His saints and to be admired IN all them that believe, (because our testimony among you was believed) in that day" II Th. 1:10 (KJ).

"Christ IN YOU, THE HOPE OF GLORY!!!" Colossians 1:28. The KJV calls it "the MYSTERY which hath been hid from ages and from generations, but now is made manifest to His saints! To whom God

63

would make known THE RICHES OF THE GLORY OF THIS MYSTERY AMONG THE GENTILES, WHICH IS . . . **CHRIST IN YOU,** THE HOPE OF GLORY!!!" The Williams translation calls this God's Glorious "OPEN SECRET — CHRIST IN YOU!!!" and Beck's Translation calls it "THE GLORY OF THIS HIDDEN TRUTH — CHRIST IN YOU!!!" I have called this, "THE KING'S GREATEST SECRET!!!!!!!!!!" Please dear Dear One, please do NOT let this truth pass you by... Please stay with this until this truth becomes nitty gritty REALITY IN YOUR GUTS. IN JESUS' Name. Amen.

So, back to the illustration — Say that Christ came into your available dead body and BECAAAAAAME it's Life, that is, started living His Glorious Life through you, loving through you, loving, talking, loving, walking, loving, living, loving, blessing, loving, healing, loving, being all that He is - in you. Being your Salvation, NOT giving you Salvation as an experience APART from Him, but living it, BE-ing, it DO-ing it through you!!

I Corinthians 1:30 says that Christ, "IS MADE unto us Wisdom, and Righteousness, and Sanctification, and Redemption". These things: Resurrection, Salvation etc., are not a "thing", or an "experience" apart from Him, but are a PERSON. That Person's Name is YAHWEH YAHSHUA, The Mighty Right Now God, The Lord and Saviour Jesus Christ!!!

Some people come staggering into church on Sunday morning to get their weakly injection fix of righteousness to last them barely till next Sunday, but

Jesus wants to BE our Righteousness!!! BE our LIFE, our Salvation and Protection. Salvation is not a "thing". Salvation is a Person! And His Name is Jesus Christ! As I John says, "He that hath the Son hath LIFE and he that hath not the Son of God hath not life."

INFERIORITY COMPLEX

They tell about a man who was down at the altar praying, "Lord, show me I'm nothing, show me I'm nothing." Then the preacher came along and said, "Take it by faith, brother." I used to have a terrible bad inferiority complex. Then somebody came along and told me I didn't have a 'feriority complex - I was just PLAIN INFERIOR!!! I used to do things constantly to "compensate" for my deep seated feelings of inadequacy. The ol' one room country school we went to was called "Wild Cat School". Then we went into town to the citified junior high school, and, truth to tell, I didn't rightly know how to act around all those city-wise kids.

So, to try to do something about my 9th grade inferiority complex, I thought maybe I could get a book from the school li-berry. The first book I got said,....... "Act natural!" But that didn't help much, you see, 'cause the thing that I "naturally" was, I knew I couldn't afford to publicly be!"

So, I got another book,.... an' it said,.... "Be yourself." But that didn't help either, because MY old self definitely WAS inferior! Later on, my friend, Lee Eliason, told me to "be sincere", and that helped some, but here, as a senior at Bethel College, my discovery of this Greatest Secret fully met the needs of my life along this line because Christ BECAME my sufficiency and my adequacy!!!!!!!! This really Really REALLY solved the problem!!!

So you don't need to die or commit suicide - because Christ wants to become your LIFE by your acceptance. Accept what He did when He took NOT ONLY our sins and sicknesses, so we can be forgiven and healed completely, but He took our SELVES. (Rom. 6, Col, Eph., etc.) He put US to death with ALL of our insufficiencies, inadequacies, inferiorities, inabilities, instabilities, everything negative, nasty, weak and sinful, and took us to the cross, put us to death, buried us and raised us up in newness of life, a whole new, beautiful, glorious, adequate, sufficient, wonderful, able, stable creation fashioned in His image, that He wants to actually BEEEEEEEEEE the Life of!!!!!!!!!

THE ELEPHANT AND THE FLEA

The story is told of an elephant that had a friend who was a flea that rode around behind his ear. They used to have lots of happy times together. One day they crossed a jungle bridge that shook, and swung and swayed. After crossing the bridge, the flea whispered into his friend's, (the elephant's) ear. Said the tiny little flea, "We sure shook that bridge didn't we!!" And at the end of each of your days, you can whisper into the Ear of your Friend, Yahweh, your Creator King, "We sure shook our world today, didn't we?" Jesus wants to beeeeeeee your LIFE!!!!!!!!!!!!!!!

67

Did you know that Christ is NOT interested in HELPING you to be righteous, or wise, or strong, or alive, apart or distant from Himself?? He wants to BEEEEEEE your Righteousness, BEEEE your Wisdom, BEEEEEEE your Strength, BEEEEEEEE your Life, BEEEEE your Everything. He doesn't want to HELP you say good words, or pray, or be disciplined, or heal, or bless, or love, as something distant or apart from Himself. He wants to pray His prayers through you by the Holy Spirit, to say His words through you, to bless with His blessing through you, to Heal with His Healing through you, to love with His love through you. Christ wants to BEEEEEEEEEEE all that He is, on location, through you!!! Do you see the difference? Do you?

THE GLORY SPELL

I was counselling with a 70 year old woman who had problems. She had a "glory spell" when I told her about the King's Greatest Secret! She said, "I was born again and baptized in the Holy Spirit when I was 10 years old and have been walking close to God ever since. But in all the 60 years I've walked with God, I've never once heard these truths, that Christ can actually BEEEEE my LIFE!!" When a person truely comes to know this wonderful Secret, then the transformation in a person's life should be just as great as if Christ Himself actually BECAAAAAAME that person's very LIFE!!! Interested?! Interested in sharing this Secret? Interested in helping us share this Secret?!

It has been tremendously exciting to share the King's Greatest Secret with so many dear ones. As of today, over 20,000 copies of this chapter have been distributed around the world, by means of our 1st book, *How To Rule The World, or Seek 1st The Kingdom Of God!*

A FOUNDATION STONE!

This Secret is so very very foundational to virtually every other truth in Scripture. For example, with regard to prayer, we must believe for Christ Himself to be on location, praying His prayers through us, according to the will of the Heavenly Father, by the power of the Holy Spirit. With regard to miracles or a ministry, we are to believe that Christ is on location, ministering and BEING that ministry through us.

So, we can have an experience GREATER THAN if we had a heart attack and Jesus Christ came into our newly dead body and started living in the earth disguised AS US, because better than this CAN BE OURS by accepting that we were crucified with Christ already on the cross in order for Him to LIVE HIS LIFE IN AND THROUGH US!!! Now He wants to BE all that He is in us, BE our life, etc. If Jesus IS our righteousness, we'll be as righteous as the Father, because Jesus is as righteous as the Father!!! Remember Jesus said in Matthew 5:48 - "BE YE THEREFORE PERFECT EVEN AS YOUR FATHER IN HEAVEN IS PERFECT." That's how we do it. Simply reckon the old life to be dead (Rom. 6), and receive Christ, not only inside to BE your Saviour and Master and total Lord, but also BEING all that He is, in you, as your Life!!! Are you ready?!!!!!!

HE wants to walk around in YOUR shoes, wearing YOUR clothes, speaking HIS words, praying HIS prayers, thinking HIS thoughts, blessing HIS people, loving, healing through you. He wants to BE the Parent of your children, the Spouse of your mate, the Worker on your job, the Child of your parents, the Friend of your friends, the Leader in your church, the Leader in your community, the Changer of your world, the Establisher of His Kingdom, the Binder and Looser of situations, the Fulfiller of the Great Commission and ALL His commandments, IN YOU and THROUGH YOU!!! (Matt 28:18-20, I John 2). ALL THIS CAN BE YOURS FROM NOW ON as CHRIST IS YOUR LIFE!! (I John 4:17). AMEN!!!!!!!

Christ wants there to be NO DIFFERENCE between who He is at the right hand of the Father and who He is - IN US!!!!! Amen!!!

If you have any question about this, leave no stone unturned until you know deeeeeeeeeep within your heart - - - this Greatest Secret of the King, if you can't get the Secret any other way please get in touch with us - because this MUST become absolutely clear to you, absolutely workable! It's the Key literally to EVERYTHING you are in God.

Instead of a crucifix, I've often thought of having a cross with nothing on it except a mirror, as a reminder that you were "there when they crucified my Lord"! And when He rose up from the grave!!!

71

Here it is then - God's Greatest Secret!!! Christ living His Glorified Life in you AS your Life!!! CHRIST LIVING HIS GLORIFIED LIFE IN YOU -IN ME - AS OUR GLORIFIED LIFE!!! This chapter - this concept - these truths - are the most important thing in this book! If I only have one chance to tell people one thing, I tell them this. The vast majority of Christians, (I would say more than 99%), do not have a working knowledge of this Greatest Secret of God. I believe that the need is so great for people to know this truth, that if you and I dedicated the rest of our entire lives to sharing this one truth, it would be worth while! What is your life being dedicated to at the present time anyway? If you are interested, let us know, or if you want a tape or the book, *How To Rule The World, or Seek 1st The Kingdom Of God,* that amplifies this truth, on "The King's Greatest Secret", or if you want to contribute to the cause, write K.O.G., P.O. 7123, Mpls., MN., 55407. Or if you want to help get this message to others, make a tax deductible check out to the Kingdom of God and send it to us. Let's make sure that this Secret, remains a 'secret' no longer!

What would happen if Christ came to the earth to live in disguise in someone before His coming in the clouds? What if He came to live His glorified Life in Your town? Your family? Your church? Your factory? Your marriage? Your shoes? Well, that's exactly what Christ wants to happen!!! Exactly! NO DIFFERENCE.

Please now let us make a prayer of II Thessalonians 1:10.

"Lord God of the impossible, now and forever, please now come and be made all glorious in me and be marvelled at in me. I believe Lord God, I believe, for You to live Your life - IN ME. Yea, BE my Life! I reckon my old life to be crucified! dead! and buried! I consider my New Life to be risen! Ascended! Seated! Glorified! and Reigning! In You, and You in me -Right Now! In THIS world! In MY life! As My Life! FROM NOW ON! And to tell this Secret to as many as possible! As quickly as possible! By whatever means possible! In as many places as possible! In Jesus Name, Amen!!

"AS CHRIST IS — SO ARE WE — IN THIS WORLD!!!"

Who would dare to put an upper limit on the marvelous possibilities of this spectacular truth!—this "Mystery of the Gospel of the Ages!, this King's Greatest Secret!?

In the Mighty Name of Yahweh Yahshua, Jesus Christ the Righteous, we insist that this Truth not be limited. Look at the above list of Scriptures again. Here are only a few in closing: 1. "I can do ALL things through Christ who strengthens me!" 2. "We...are transformed into God's very same image!!!" 3. "The works that I do shall you do, and greater works than these shall ye do!!" 4. "Even as He walks!!" 5. "AS HE IS - SO ARE WE -IN THIS WORLD!!!!!"

HOW TO BE A PERFECT PARENT!!!

If God stepped down from a fleecy white cloud and offered to give to you a pill that you could take or a simple plan to follow that would enable you to be a

73

"perfect parent", would you be interested?? Many would not, because they want to hang on to their excuses for NOT being a perfect parent. Well, this chapter just told you how, very simply, YOU CAN BE THE KIND OF PARENT GOD WANTS YOU TO BE!!! Furthermore, you can, by following the truths outlined in this chapter, teach your children "How To Be Perfect" also. How about it? Are you willing to give it a try? Or, have you "taken it by faith" that it is impossible? Write, and let us know how you are getting along.

Now, let's look at one of the things that might happen if your friends learn this Secret.

REVIEW QUESTIONS — CHAPTER 4

1. Is it possible to live without sinning? (Explain).
2. What of ours did Christ take with Him to the cross?
3. What is God's greatest secret?
4. What is the difference between Christ helping you do or speak good things & Him speaking or doing good things through you?
5. Why was it necessary for Christ to take you with Him to the cross?
6. Without a practical revelation understanding of the King's Greatest Secret, does positive thinking have much power?
7. Why is suicide not necessary?
8. What Scripture verses go with the following phrases (you may look them up from the list of Scriptures provided below):
   Victory _____, Victory always everywhere _____, Free from sin _____, Risen with Christ our life _____, Seated in Christ _____, Fullness of joy: joy unspeakable _____, Every blessing _____, Joy of the Lord —strength _____, Mind of Christ _____, Can do all things through Christ _____, Walk

blamelessly _____, All power and authority _____, We are the light of the World _____, To live is Christ _____, All power and authority _____, What ever we ask _____, Abundant Life _____, We have all things for life _____, More than conquerors _____, We can be as He is _____, All things are possible _____, We can walk as He walked _____, Greater works _____ , We can know the mysteries of the Kingdom of God. The Mystery of the Gospel of the ages _____, Christ is made unto us, Wisdom _____

Jude 24; Ph. 1:21; Eph. 1:3,4; Rom. 8:37; Col. 3:1-3; II Cor.2:14-16; Matt. 5:14; II Pet. 1:1-4; John 14:13; Ps. 16:11; Rom. 6:7,18,22; Ph. 4:13; Ne. 8:10; Eph. 2:6; I Cor. 15:57; Cor. 2:16; Matt. 28:18; II Cor. 9:8; I Cor. 1:30; Luke 8:10; I John 4:17; John 10:10; John 14:12; Mat. 19:26; Col.1:25-29; I John 2:6.

9. Gal.2:20 - Are you living?
10. Can we be perfect?
11. What did Jesus mean when He said, "Be perfect!"? (Matt.5:48).
12. How can we be perfect?
13. What is the main solution for most arguments about the Bible?
14. How is "calling 'idealistic' what God calls necessary and practical" - calling God a liar?
15. What 3 steps are necessary for Christ to be your Life?
16. Do you have the mind of Christ?

17. In the Word, what's the main evidence, sign, fruit, or proof that you are full of God?

18. Not "have" you been filled with, but are you full of God right now? (Give yourself a percentage)

19. What would happen to a clean and freshly sacrificed (killed) lamb under the hot Israel sun if nothing more happened after it was killed?

20. What else is necessary?

21. What is this symbolic of?

22. Who should praise the Lord with shouting & clapping? (Ps.47).

23. Why can we have an experience MORE REAL than if we fell dead and Christ was looking around for a fresh warm dead body He could move into and raise up and become the Life of, living on the earth again - disguised as you?

24. Who is the flea—the elephant, in the illustration?

25. What is the main difference between Christ helping us do or be something, and Him being or doing it in and through us?

26. Are we supposed to discipline the old nature or the old self?

27. Does Christ want there to be any difference between who He is at the Father's right hand & who He is - in us?

28. If you devoted the rest of your life to sharing this Secret - would your life be well spent?

29. Will you?

30. Do you think it is possible to "Raise Perfect Children"?

31. Is it possible to be a perfect parent?

5

THE ALTITUDE OF OUR ATTITUDE

At this point, we would like to apply the truths presented in the last chapter to our attitudes toward one another in the family of God, in general and to your family specifically. Please bear with us as we endeavor to lay a foundation. The implications are "fantabulous"!

What would happen if Christ became the life of the mother of your children? The father? What would happen if Christ became the Life of your child(ren)? Then - IT WOULD BECOME ACCREDITED TO THE ACCOUNT OF EVERYONE ELSE, THE WAY EACH ONE RELATED TO THAT PERSON THAT CHRIST HAD BECOME THE LIFE OF!!!

Remember when Jesus talked about this?

We have defined Kingdom anarchy as being: "Any ONE or any THING that rejects or fails to cooperate with anyone the King sends or anything that the King directs or desires."

Remember the story of the excited woman who had been promised a visit at her house from the King in person? When only a child, a poor beggar and an old man appeared during that day, she was disappointed and next day asked the King why He did not come. He said, "I did come, but I was disguised as a child, a poor beggar, and an old man, and do you remember how you received me?"

Consider the following Scriptural examples of Kingdom Relating:

1. Matthew 18:1-10 (1) "At that time the disciples came up and asked Jesus, 'Who then is [really] the greatest in the Kingdom of Heaven?' (or Kingdom of God). (2) And He called a little child to Him and put him in the midst of them, (3) And said 'Truly, I say to you, unless you repent and become like little children [trusting, lowly, loving, forgiving] you can NEVER enter the Kingdom of Heaven at all. (4) Whoever will humble himself therefore, and becomes as this little child, is greatest in the Kingdom of Heaven; (5) And WHOEVER RECEIVES AND ACCEPTS and welcomes ONE LITTLE CHILD LIKE THIS for My sake and in My Name RECEIVES and ACCEPTS AND WELCOMES ME! (6) But whoever causes one of these little ones who believe and acknowledge and cleave to Me to stumble and sin - that is, who entices him, or hinders him in right conduct or thought - it would be better (more expedient and profitable or advantageous) for him to have a great millstone fastened around his neck and to be sunk in the depth of the sea. (7) Woe to the world for such temptations to sin and influences to do wrong! It is necessary that temptations come, but WOE to the person on whose account or by whom the temptation comes! (8) And if

your hand or your foot causes you to stumble and sin, pluck it out and throw it away from you; it is better, more profitable and wholesome) for you to enter life with only one eye than with two eyes be thrown into the hell of fire. (10) Beware that you do not despise or feel scornful toward or think little of one of these little ones, for I tell you that in Heaven their angels always are in the presence of and look upon the Face of My Father Who is in Heaven."' (AMP).

2. Matt. 10:40 "He who receives you receives Me, and he who receives Me receives Him who sent Me." v. 41 "He who receives a prophet in the name of a prophet shall receive a prophet's reward." The question I have is, "WHAT HAPPENS IF we reject the prophet or reject the righteous man, or REFUSE TO GIVE TO ONE OF THE LITTLE ONES A CUP OF COLD WATER, or refuse to give to our Kingdom brother that asks of us??? And now the rest of verses 41 and 42, " and he who receives a righteous man in the name of a righteous man shall receive a righteous man's reward. And WHOEVER IN THE NAME OF A DISCIPLE GIVES TO ONE OF THESE LITTLE ONES [or humble folk] even a cup of cold water to drink, truly I say to you he shall not lose his reward."

3. Luke 10:16 "The one who listens to you listens to Me, and the one who rejects you rejects Me; and he who rejects Me rejects the One who sent Me." How about putting this in our promise box and our memory pack? And how about putting our brother or sister who is doing the will of God in the verse?

4. The parable of the sheep and the goats: "Then

the King will say to those on His right, 'Come, you who are blessed of My Father, inherit the Kingdom prepared for you from the foundation of the world" (Matt. 25:34). These got into the Kingdom of God because they gave food, clothing, and shelter to those who are doing the Father's will! "And the King will answer and say to them, Truly, I say to you, to the extent that you did it to one of these brothers of Mine, even the least of them, you did it TO ME!!" (Matt. 25:40) The reason the others went to hell's "eternal fire" was because they did NOT give food, clothing, and shelter to those who were doing the will of God. "Then He will answer them, saying, 'Truly, I say to you, to the extent that you did not do it to ONE OF THE LEAST OF THESE you did not do it TO ME'!!! And these will go away into ETERNAL punishment, but the righteous into eternal life" (Matt. 12:45-46). Perhaps you may be asking, "To whom does 'the least of these My brothers' refer?" Jesus, Himself answered that question in Matthew 12:46-50, "While He was still speaking to the multitudes, behold, His mother and His brothers were standing outside, seeking to speak to Him. And someone said to Him, "Behold, your mother and your brothers are standing outside seeking to speak to You.' But He answered the one who was telling Him and said, "Who is My mother and who are My brothers?' And stretching out His hand toward His disciples, He said, "Behold, My mother and My brothers! For WHOEVER SHALL DO THE WILL OF MY FATHER Who is in Heaven,

81

he IS MY BROTHER AND SISTER AND MOTHER.' " Also in Luke 8:20,21, "But He (Jesus) answered and said unto them, 'My mother and My brothers are THESE WHO HEAR THE WORD OF GOD AND DO IT' ".

JUDGING WITH UNRIGHTEOUS JUDGEMENT

One of the cruelest and meanest things I ever did as a father was to spank our Darling Dawn Joy when she did not deserve it. We were new to the neighborhood, and Dawn decided to ride her bike around the block. A neighbor girl, who was blocking the sidewalk, took offense when Dawn asked her to move out of the way. She then pretended to be Dawn's friend and asked her to go for a ride with her. But when they got to the other end of the block, the neighbor girl and her friends threw Dawn Joy down and beat her up, pulling out hands full of hair, simply because Dawn had asked this girl to move, when she was blocking the way. When I went to investigate the beating, I was confronted by a number of black people who accused Dawn Joy of calling this neighbor girl a "nigger". It was their word against hers, so I kept interrogating Dawn until she finally admitted to their accusation. So, in front of these people, I took a flexible green switch, and gave Dawn a switching, for three reasons: 1. Because she had initially lied, 2. Because of her racial slur, and, 3. To appease the indignation of the neighbors. BUT, LATER, I FOUND OUT THAT I WAS WRONG!!! I found out later, that, in fact, Dawn Joy had NOT called her neighbor girl any names, and

82

had NOT acted disrespectfully. Dawn only had admitted to the accusation because she was hurting, confused and afraid, not only of the neighbors, but of me. I have many times, asked Dawn Joy to forgive me, and each time, she, of course sweetly has. This heartbreaking lesson has taught us to never ever falsely accuse or punish unless we know absolutely, beyond any shadow of doubt...

THE REAL ENEMY

Here is a very important Kingdom Principle to REMEMBER: "We wrestle not against flesh and blood, but against principalities, against powers, against the rulers of the dark-ness of this world, against spiritual wickedness in high places" Eph. 6:12 (KJ).

The following illustrations include several ways in which the defeated enemy tries to bring division and separation and misunderstanding within the family and in the body of Christ:

LAUREL & HARDY - ABBOT & COSTELLO

Remember in the cartoons or movies where two friends are walking along when a third person jumps out from hiding and hits one of the two friends. The hit friend, seeing no one but his friend, assumes that this friend hit him, and says to himself, "I can't let my friend hit me for no good reason." So he hauls off and hits his friend, who says, "I can't let my friend hit me for no good reason." So they are fighting while the enemy is full of glee, still in hiding. It's funny in the cartoons, but not so funny in the family or marriage or in church or among friends.

INVISIBLE WEDGE SHAPED PRINCIPALITIES

Imagine that the enemy would sometimes send an invisible wedge shaped principality between you and your friend. If you are not discerning, you may assume that the problem is coming from your family member or friend, and/or your friend from you.

PASS THE TOAST - TWISTER SPIRIT

Imagine a husband and wife sitting at breakfast when the husband says to her, "Pass the toast." But what he really means is "Darling, I love you so much, I can hardly wait to get home from work to see you, you sweet thing, you are so precious, I'm so glad I married you, and, by the way, would you purty please pass me the toast?" But, remember, all he said was, "Pass the toast." (Maybe he was still waking up.) But suppose she got the wrong impression and that the enemy twisted the intent of his message so that by the time it reached her ears she assumed that he meant, "Hey, you old bag, pass me the toast before I hit you in the mouth." She responds by saying, "WHADDYA MEAN, 'PASS THE TOAST?' GIDITCHERSELF." I've seen this kind of thing happen often in people's interpersonal relationships. But in this illustration, suppose that the husband meant something negative, but because of her love and her trust and her faith, she responded sweetly by saying, "Oh darling, I love you too, you precious sweet thing you, and I can hardly wait to see you, and by the way, here's the toast for my honey." (See our book on THE LOVE MINISTRY.) For even though he may have originally meant something negative, he can't help but respond to her faith and trust and love. Get the picture? This same breakdown in communication can take place also with the children.

HITCHHIKER SPIRIT

We have a friend that people would become aggravated with for no apparent reason. People would want to haul off and hit poor Richard even though he had done nothing to cause this kind of reaction. Finally, a man of God discerned that the enemy had sent a spirit of aggravation to follow this person to create this kind of reaction in people. Richard was actually a very friendly guy.

IT'S CURTAINS FOR THE ENEMY

Sometimes this situation exists in circles or in waves or curtains around a person especially called of God or chosen of God for a special work or ministry, and usually to the extent of that ministry's importance in the Kingdom of God. In every case, the LORD HAS GIVEN US POWER OVER THE ENEMY, TO TAKE AUTHORITY OVER THE SITUATION. But in this illustration, when approaching a person, one may feel reactions of rejection, lust, hate, isolation, arrogance, aggravation, confusion, or deception. It is important to KNOW THE PERSON'S HEART because these conditions may only exist in the atmosphere around a person who is called of God and who is, in fact, a loving, accepting, humble, anointed man or woman of God. Sometimes, unless a person is very sharp in discerning, one may interpret

85

THE INVISIBLE WEDGE-SHAPED
PRINCIPALITY

LAUREL & HARDY // ABBOT & COSTELLO

as coming from another person something that in reality is not in that person's heart, or being.

Remember: THE ENEMY IS ALWAYS TRYING TO MAKE LOOK BAD WHAT'S GOOD AND TO MAKE LOOK GOOD WHAT'S BAD so that it is always necessary to move in a state of KINGDOM REVELATION or DISCERNMENT. "Evil men do not understand justice, but THOSE WHO SEEK THE LORD UNDERSTAND ALL THINGS" Pr. 28:5. Remember — it's the revelation gifts of knowledge, discernment, wisdom — NOT the gift of suspicion! We've known folks who thought of themselves as being spiritual when in fact they were religiously suspicious and doubting.

A man of God has said that he would rather err in trusting love and be wrong by having trusted with faith and love as a basis 999 times, than to be wrong 1 time in 1000 through unrighteous judging, with suspicion and unbelief as it's wrong basis.

SELECTED SCRIPTURES ON BEING RIGHTLY RELATED

1. Matthew, Mark and Luke all refer to this one, but we'll quote Jesus in Matt. 18:3-6, "Truly I say to you, unless you are converted and become like children, you shall not enter the Kingdom of Heaven. Whoever then humbles himself as this child, he is the greatest in the Kingdom of Heaven. And whoever receives one such child in My Name receives Me; But whoever causes one of these little ones who believes in Me to stumble, it would be better for him that a

87

millstone were hanged about his neck, and that he were drowned in the depths of the sea." The children referred to here are not only little children, but it is also talking about the humble citizens of the Kingdom, those who do the Father's will.

2) Matt. 5:19-24, "Whosoever therefore shall break one of these least commandments, and shall teach men so, he shall be called the least in the Kingdom of Heaven: but whosoever shall do and teach them, the same shall be called great in the Kingdom of Heaven. For I say unto you, that except your righteousness shall exceed the righteousness of the scribes and Pharisees, ye shall in no case enter into the Kingdom of Heaven. Ye have heard that it was said by them of old time, 'Thou shalt not kill; and whosoever shall kill shall be in danger of the judgment': but I say unto you, that whosoever is angry with his brother without a cause shall be in danger of the judgment: and whosoever shall say to his brother, 'Raca', ['good for nothing'] shall be in danger of the council: but whosoever shall say, 'Thou fool', shall be in danger of hell fire. Therefore if thou bring thy gift to the altar, and there rememberest that thy brother hath ought against thee; leave there thy gift before the altar, and go thy way; first be reconciled to thy brother, and then come and offer thy gift." (KJ)

3) I John 3:14-18, "We know that we have passed from death unto life, because we love the brethren. He that loveth not his brother abideth in death. Whosoever hateth his brother is a murderer: and ye know that no murderer hath eternal life abiding in

him. Hereby perceive we the love of God, because he laid down his life for us: and we ought to lay down our lives for the brethren. But whoso hath this world's good, and seeth his brother have need, and shutteth up his heart of compassion from him, how dwelleth the love of God in him? My little children, let us not love in word, neither in tongue (only); but in deed and in truth." (KJ)

I John 4:20-21, "If a man say, 'I love God,' and hateth his brother, he is a liar: for he that loveth not his brother whom he hath seen, how can he love God whom he hath not seen? And this commandment have we from him, That he who loveth God love his brother also." (KJ)

It is right to be outraged at the Atlanta Murderer, or the Nazi slaughters, but we need to feel equal outrage at the spiritual, psychic, emotional, or mental murders and assaults and torments WE members of the body of Christ commit against each other as husbands, wives, brothers, sisters, family members, pastors, evangelists, members of the body of Christ — and especially the 'humble ones' who are trying earnestly to fulfill the will of God and the Great Commission —The brothers and sisters and mothers of Christ. When Paul was persecuting the Christians, Jesus said, "Why are you persecuting Me?" (Acts 9:4b) and "I am Jesus whom you are persecuting" (vs 5).

HOW TO HAVE WISDOM

Here is a sure-fire way to have wisdom. I Corinthians 1:30 tells us that Jesus Christ - Yeshua the Messiah, IS our Wisdom: "Jesus Christ IS MADE unto us WISDOM." Again, Jesus Christ is not interested in giving us little shots of wisdom, HE WANTS TO BE OUR WISDOM!!!

Here is a sure-fire way to have wisdom. I Corinthians 1:30 tells us that Jesus Christ — Yashua the Messiah, IS our Wisdom: "Jesus Christ IS MADE unto us WISDOM." Again, Jesus Christ is not interested in giving us little shots of wisdom, HE WANTS TO BE OUR WISDOM!!!

With this concept in mind, we welcome you to read the Book of Proverbs again, remembering that wisdom is not a "thing" — Wisdom is a Person. And His Name is Yeshuah — Jesus!!!

Consider this fact as you consider these Scriptures, if you want to be a good parent — Let Jesus Christ Himself BE the Parent of your child(ren), and BE the Wisdom of your life!

"That your faith should not rest on the wisdom of men, but on the power of God. Yet we do speak wisdom among those who are mature; a wisdom, however, not of this age, nor of the rulers of this age, who are passing away;

"But we speak God's wisdom in a mystery, the hidden wisdom, which God predestined before the ages to our glory;

"The wisdom which none of the rulers of this age has understood; for if they had understood it, they would not have crucified the Lord of glory;

"But just as it is written, 'Things which eye has not seen and ear has not heard, and which have not

90

entered the heart of man, all that God has prepared for those who love Him.'

"For to us God revealed them through the Spirit; for the Spirit searches all things, even the depths of God.

"For who among men knows the thoughts of a man except the spirit of the man which is in him? Even so the thoughts of God no one knows except the Spirit of God.

Now we have received, not the spirit of the world, but the Spirit who is from God that we might know the things freely given to us by God.

"Which things we also speak, not in words taught by human wisdom, but in those taught by the Spirit, combining spiritual thoughts with spiritual words.

"But a natural man does not accept the things of the Spirit of God; for they are foolishness to him, and he cannot understand them, because they are spiritually appraised.

"BUT HE WHO IS SPIRITUAL (not unspiritual) APPRAISES ALL THINGS, YET HE HIMSELF IS APPRAISED BY NO MAN.

"For who has known the Mind of the Lord that he should instruct Him? But we have the Mind of Christ" I Cor. 2:5-16.

Job's wife and his friends were wrong. Eli the priest was wrong with Samuel's mother. David's brothers were wrong when he wanted to kill Goliath. Saul was wrong when he wanted to kill David. REMEMBER: A DECEIVED PERSON NEVER KNOWS WHEN HE OR SHE IS DECEIVED. And you may be wrong also! Remember: the greatest key to knowing the will of God is to have a deep Deep DEEP commitment to **DO** THE WILL OF GOD!!! John 7:17

I ask again, do you know all there is to know about God? We don't either. But can we agree to be patient with each other in this marvelous adventure of being led into all truth by the Holy Spirit?

"I praise Thee, O Father, Lord of heaven and earth, that Thou didst hide these things from the wise and intelligent, and didst reveal them to babes." Luke 10:21.

God be merciful to all of us as we seek diligently to please Him in everything.

Romans 14 is good in this regard. Now we are NOT talking about things in the Bible that God has clearly said are sin. But there are a multitude of other areas where we are guilty of judging. Verse 4, "Who art thou that judgest another man's servant? To his own master he standeth or falleth." (KJ)

So, we see that there is such a deep need for us to love each other unconditionally, without criticism or walls, or character assassination or resentment. The Lord says that it is not enough to love one another tolerantly, but that we are to "obey the truth through the Spirit unto unfeigned love of the brethren, see that ye Love One Another With A Pure Heart Fervently!!!" (I Peter 1:22).

We worship You, Oh Lord God of the Universe, Lord Jesus Christ and we also will be careful to honor You, and appreciate You, in our brother and in our sister! We repent for not having rightly related to You in the least of the brothers and sisters, and especially in the members of our own family, and ask that by your grace we will always rightly relate to You wherever You are found.

We ask you Lord Jesus for the Spirit of Wisdom, Revelation and the Knowledge of our God to rest upon us, unceasingly — increasingly. Yea Lord, Be our Life. BE OUR WISDOM! Live within us AS the Parent of our child(ren). Love through us with a pure and fervent practical I Cor. 13 and I John type of love. We dedicate our home to be Your home, our property to be Your property. Our house, our family IS a part of Your Kingdom. Therefore we receive Your Great Commission that our home be Your Home and that our kingdom be Your Kingdom. We pray, "Thy Kingdom come — Thy will be done in our house — in our family —as it is in Heaven."

In Jesus Christ's Name we pray and believe, Amen.

REVIEW QUESTIONS - CHAPTER 5

1. Complete this thought, "it is accredited to our account as having been done to Christ, the way _____."

2. Who is our wisdom?

3. Rather than that we offend "one of these little ones" what would be better?

4. If we call someone a fool, or an idiot, or stupid, what are we in danger of?

5. Is it possible to be a perfect parent?

6. If so, how?

7. If we receive a little child in Jesus' name, who do we receive?

8. Complete this thought: "The devil is always trying to make _____ look good and to make _____ look bad.

9. Pleast try to explain these following illustrations:
   A. Laurel & Hardy/Abbot and Costello:

   B. The invisible wedged shaped principalities:

   C. Pass the toast:

   D. Curtains for the enemy:

6

THE UNCONDITIONAL KEYS
TO THE KEYS

I have told my children that my love for them will remain strong, no matter what they do, because I want them to know that my love for them is unconditional. I believe that this will provide the basis for an even greater walk with God for them than if I only had the kind of love that worked when they were on top.

For example, I have told my daughters that if they were to become prostitutes or marry someone of whom we disapprove, that we will still love them, dearly deeply love them, no matter how much they hurt us - because our love for each other must not have conditions attached to it. I have told my sons that my love for them is not based upon their right behavior but is unconditional, even if they were to become criminal.

Now, you may be thinking that this kind of love would be giving license or encouragement for them to act destructively. On the contrary, this kind of love actually sets them free to love and live sacrificially toward us and God in response.

God has given to us many dear friends who are mighty gifts of God to be with us in the fulfillment of God's Great Commission. (YOU ARE WELCOME, TOO!!!) These people and their families have made the difference in the realization of God's destiny. David has provided countless hours of computer service. John has provided much help mechanically. Frank has been a blessing with the tapes; Jerry with food; Audrey with prayer, others have given money, the Dodges have been dear friends, etc., etc. But these people all know that our love for them is NOT the result of their ministry to us, but that our love for them will be as strong if they rejected us or even hated us. This realization causes them to love us even more, because it has no "strings" attached. I don't serve God because I "have to". I serve Him because I want to — and the most exquisite privilege imaginable!!! Grand and glorious — adventuring in Him — day by day. I turned to Karen when we were in Israel last year, and said, "Sweetheart, I just want to serve Him for love's dear sake alone!" And, she agreed!

Recently, my wife was in Europe for a month. Her friends lovingly remarked about all the love-letters I wrote to her. One such letter had been written with ink that wasn't waterproof, and each of the 12 pages had tear drop smears on them — tears of love —tears of deep appreciation. In my letter to her, I reassured her of my love, reminding her that my love for her was "unconditional", that is, not based on any kind or quality of love's return on her part. (She does love me, by the way —wonderfully — but she loves me first of all because — she is FREE to love me. She does not love me because I'll hit her in the mouf' if she doesn't. I'll love her if she doesn't love me!)

God says, "But I say unto you which hear, love your enemies, do good to them which hate you. ...For if ye love them which love you, what thank have ye? For sinners also love those that love them. ...But love your enemies, and do good, and lend, hoping for nothing again; and YOUR REWARD SHALL BE GREAT, and YE SHALL BE CALLED CHILDREN OF THE HIGHEST: for He is kind unto the unthankful and to the evil. Be therefore merciful, as your Father is also merciful!!!" St. Luke 6 & Matthew 5.

A PROSTITUTE?

How many parents, husbands, wives and friends have the kind of love that says, directly or indirectly, "I'll love you IF....." That's what a prostitute is, male or female. They give "love" IF... IF they are paid, or IF they receive some kind of favor or benefit. Are you this kind of person? Is this the kind of love you have? I refuse to allow my friends and family to be "prostituted" on my account. And I refuse to be a "prostitute". Therefore, I want to love freely; want to receive love without "paying" for it. I love you.

FOREVER IS A LONG LONG TIME TO BURN

By the way, we do not mean that God will forgive us no matter what we do. God has a problem in that He is Holy, Righteous, Just, Pure and Good. Not that that is a problem, but it is not possible for Him to

97

fellowship with those who are full of spiritual pus and vomit. As it were, God's sense of smell is too keen to stand the hideous stinking putrefaction arising from some people's mouths and lives, so He has made provision for our perfect cleansing!

In the Old Testament, I have noticed that there are many sacrifices and offerings for "unintentional sin", but I cannot find any provision of His grace for "INTENTIONAL SIN." I John says, "He that sins is of his father, the devil." Some folks think that they can play around with sin in the Presence of a Holy God, but the New Testament says that "Is a fearful thing to fall into the Hands of the Living God" and "Our God is a Consuming Fire!" and "Without holiness, no man shall see the Lord." and "Be ye therefore perfect, even as your Father in Heaven is perfect."! And, please keep in mind that this perfection, righteousness and holiness is NOT theoretical only but absolutely MUST BE practical, gut-level and "where we live"!

God says, "Therefore if any man (or person) be in Christ, he (or she), is a new creature: old things are passed away; behold all things become new." "For He hath made Him who knew no sin, to be sin FOR US, that we might be MADE THE RIGHTEOUSNESS OF GOD IN HIM!!!" II Corinthians 5.

All that's needed is that we accept the pardon by inviting Jesus Christ into our life, turning the whole blessed mess over to Him completely, receive Him as our Savior, Lord and Life, do what He says from now on, and live happily ever after!!!

But if we refuse the pardon and the provision, then God Almighty Himself cannot help us, therefore He will not. A God of love, He will not force you to love Him, to be with Him, and where He's not — is hell. And hell is hot. And forever is a l o n g, loooooooooonnng time to burn! But, you may go there if you like. But we don't recommend it this time of year, or any other.

If you would like to have more information on the subject of hell, please write to us at K.O.G., P.O. 7123, Minneapolis, MN., 55407.

Some folks say, "If God is a God of Love, He wouldn't send people to hell, (or any other uncomfortable place)." But LOVE PRESUPPOSES THE NECESSITY OF CHOICE! And God will not force you to love Him, though He pleads for you. Hell is the other choice. Aw, go to - - - HEAVEN!!! It's really possible to live HAPPILY EVER AFTER!!!

REVIEW QUESTIONS — CHAPTER 6

1. Would you still love your child if he or she became a prostitute?

2. What is meant by, "Love without strings attached"?

3. Will God Himself keep us from hell if we really want to go there?

4. How hot is hell?

5. How long will hell last?

6. Will God forgive you if you don't repent?

PART II

7

THE KEYS

In this chapter, we would like to discuss some practical keys, or Kingdom Principles having to do with raising "purfect" children. We hope earnestly that they will be a blessing to you or yours.

1. WHY PRAY (or play) WHEN YOU CAN WORRY?

At our house, it is such a grand and glorious adventure to walk with God together, praying, playing, adventuring, singing, loving each other, having family meetings, church in the home often with just our family or perhaps a handful of others. I can't begin to describe the lovely times we have. In a small family meeting, everyone has a chance to pray, read Scriptures aloud, sing in the spirit, ask questions, listen to each other or otherwise share. What growth, what enjoyment! We treasure these times together. Or when riding along the way, we sing and share and pray together. I asked Joshua once, what was his happiest moment of his life. He replied, "When I am singing to Jesus for people!" But what ingredients

101

specifically work to help with such a happy atmosphere? We would like for you to listen carefully to these following points.

2. "ONLY SAY 'NO' ONE TIME!"
or
AT WHAT POINT DID YOU MEAN THE 'NO' YOU SAID?

When our oldest son was still a baby, I became a probation officer with Los Angeles County, just after the Watts riots and during the East Los Angeles and Santa Barbara riots. For several of those years, I worked in a juvenile hall setting where I was in charge of the daily care of perhaps 30 boys or young men ranging anywhere from 7 to 19 years of age. I quickly learned that my survival as a probation officer depended upon the successful application of these principles, as a surrogate or substitute parent among kids that mostly hated authority of any kind.

One such principle was this. ONLY SAY 'NO' ONE TIME!!! Now you may think this is ridiculous, but any other policy is even more ridiculous. Picture me in a juvenile hall dayroom setting, alone with 30 hostile 17 and 18 year old murderers, thugs, thieves and liars, etc. and we've got to get over to the dining hall, with its dishes, food, glasses, forks, and knives. When I say, "Let's line it up at the door", and they look at me like I'm some kind of jive turkey, honkey, gringo dude what don' got his act together. Brother, I had BETTER have my act together quick or I got a riot on my hands and some body's likely to get hurt, maybe even me! If I give everybody a second chance to be taking care of business in their own sweet time, that's 60 mess ups, before the point gets across.

By now you may be saying, "What has that got to do with me. We know a multitude of couples who say "no" as many times as it is that they normally say no before they finally get around to meaning business. Little Johnny, (the name has been changed to protect the guilty) reaches for the vase of pretty flowers. Mom says "No, no, no Johnny." Whereupon Johnny gives her his best 3 year old "Boyoboy Mom, ain't I just the cutest thing ?" - look, and stretches forth his hand again to the pretty, (and expensive) vase. Whereupon Mommie says, "Now cutie pie dearest thing poopsie, Mommie told you not to touch. NO NO". And so the game goes until the child wins and everybody loses including the child, and the vase gets broken, and the child gets hurt, and Mommie gets angry, and the flowers got ruined and the child learned that Dearest Mommie's "No" meant "maybe", or "perhaps" or "yes" or "probably" or "Go on do what you blessed well please."

Some would recommend that one simply should put everything out of reach. But what happens when the child happens to get around something that CAN be reached? We had four teen-agers in our family this year, though now they just turned 14, 16, 18, & 20. We have never put things out of "reach"; we just simply taught them the meaning of the little word "no". Now they are assuming adult responsibilities, and there is a whole universe of things they can "reach". But they were intelligent enough to learn what this little word meant even at the age of 6 months or before. Now they are grown, or nearly so, and they have not forgotten. We also taught them what the word "yes" means, and we did not have to "break their spirits" to teach them either word. How significant are the words of God, (aren't they all?) when He said, "Let your 'yes' be 'yes', and your 'no' be 'no'."

But, in the example given above, the mother should have said "no" only one time and then for God's and everybody else's sake have stepped in and taught the cute little darling the fear of God. Otherwise you are training and teaching him that you or any other authority, including God, do not mean business, that your "No" means "perhaps" and that your "yes" probably means "probably not". The saying is, "But let your communication be, Yea, yea; Nay, nay: for whatsoever is more than these cometh of evil." Matthew 5:37.

3. SHOULD THE CHILD BE SPANKED? or "APPLYING THE BOARD OF EDUCATION TO THE SEAT OF LEARNING" or AIN'T THAT A SWITCH!

Here again, we would like to recommend that you take the Book of Proverbs and make special note of all that it says about discipline. In so doing you are getting the Lord's opinion directly, without going through Dear Aunt Frannie or Uncle Schmock. If you do, you'll get the distinct impression that the Lord is indeed in favor of discipline! Repeated reference is made to "the rod", and comes from the Hebrew word "shebet" meaning a branch or a stick and carries with it the idea of a flexible green switch, and not a club.

4. NOT RECOMMENDING EITHER KIND OF ABUSE

We have a dear friend named Audrey, that may be the subject of a fifth book we are writing, who was repeatedly tortured and cruelly beaten with fire-wood and clubs as a child, and we are believing for the curse of Almighty God upon this kind of cruelty. In fact, Audrey's mother actually did die, while Audrey was praying, "Lord, I don't think I can take any more. Please help me." Audrey is our dear dear friend, and we are not advocating mutilation or mistreatment. But there is another kind of cruelty—one of a parent that fails to discipline—that also results in crime, misery and heartache. I've seen by the hundreds those that have NOT been disciplined, and they have grown up to lie, steal, cheat, and kill, all because of that other kind of cruel cruelty that FAILED to discipline in the love of God.

I have heard that in Sweden, it is against the law for a parent to spank or even scold the child, and the suicide rate among those children is terrifying! Guess why?

5. SELECTED VERSES ON DISCIPLINE FROM THE BOOK OF PROVERBS

3:11,12 "My son, despise not the chastening of the Lord: neither be weary of His correction:"

105

"For whom the Lord loveth He correcteth; even as a father in whom he delighteth."

13:24 "He that spareth his rod, (switch or stick) hateth his son: but he that loveth him chasteneth him betimes."

19:18 "Chasten thy son while there is hope, and let not thy soul spare for his crying."

22:6,15 "Train up a child in the way he should go: and when he is old, he will not depart from it." "Foolishness (rebellion) is bound in the heart of a child; but the rod (switch or stick) of correction shall drive it far from him."

23:13,14 "Withhold not correction from the child: for if thou beatest him with the rod, (switch or stick), he shall not die."

"Thou shalt beat him with the rod (switch or stick), and shall deliver his soul from hell."

"The rod and reproof give wisdom: but a dchild left to himself bringeth his mother to shame." "Correct thy son, and he shall give thee rest; yea, he shall give delight unto thy soul."

6. A GENTLE WORD OF CAUTION

What we are advocating here is the sanctified, loving, Spirit led use of a flexible green switch, or stick, of less thickness than a pencil. Here's why. Care must be taken that the child is not injured while being disciplined. For example, a hair brush, or wooden spoon, or a board, or ruler, or yard stick, or ping pong paddle can all bruise hip bones, tail bones, knee bones, finger, hand, arm or wrist bones or the back. And if not used properly can also bruise muscles, nerves or tendons. Although the child must be taught to not fight the discipline, sometimes there is the inevitable squirming around or the reaction to the pain which can cause the paddle to miss the mark. So this is why we advocate the use of a flexible narrow switch.

7. DON'T RAISE YOUR VOICE.

Here we are encouraging that you do not raise your voice or get into the habit of yelling unless it's a "voice raising" situation. If you do get into the habit of raising your voice or yelling to indicate you mean business then you are training-teaching the child that you do not mean business until the point that you begin hollering.

We have taught our children to respond to a glance or an almost imperceptible nod or gesture across a crowded room of hundreds of people. They know that if they go beyond that point and ignore the gesture, or nod, or look, that the fear of God will happen all over them. If this training did not start at an early age, which is by far the best, then it must start now.

Suppose you are sitting in church and the child feels like misbehaving. The clever little tyke is smart enough to know that it will cause you inconvenience for you to discipline him. But this is really an important time to teach him that the discipline is sure and will be certainly more severe because of the inconvenience. He is smart enough to know also that he will not be allowed to get by with this kind of thing in the future. But if you allow him to get by with this now, you will be paying for this neglect with heavy interest until this lesson is learned, if ever.

8. ALWAYS DISCIPLINE TO THE POINT OF REPENTANCE.

Many parents discipline their children only to the point where they have a wrong spirit or wrong attitude. Let's say the parents have graduated to the point where they are using a flexible green switch. So they take the switch and go "thwak, thwak, thwak," and then stop. Most children are disciplined for a wrong action, and much of the time, they will still have a wrong spirit, heart attitude or reaction when the discipline is finished. When a parent allows this to happen, they are teaching the child that it is o.k. for them to have a wrong attitude.

We are recommending what we believe to be a wiser approach. We suggest that after three or four thwaks, (switchs with the switch) that you stop and check the child's heart attitude or spirit to see if it is positive. Chances are, however, that you will notice rebellion, anger, bitterness, withdrawal, or self-pity, etc. At this point we encourage you to tell the child to get his spirit right by saying something like, "stop being rebellious", or, "stop being angry", or, "don't pout". If he does not immediately get his spirit right, then give him three or four more licks with the switch.

Then stop and check his spirit. If it is not right or his attitude is not one of repentance, tell him again to get his spirit right. If it is not immediately corrected, switch him again.

We strongly recommend that you continue this process until the child's spirit and attitude and reaction reflect tenderness and repentance.

Across the miles I can hear the cries of protest from child and parent alike about this point. But look at this. Unless the above recommendation is followed, you are training the child to react with negative intensity. But if this recommendation is followed, you are training the child:

1. CONTROL OVER HIS OWN SPIRIT "He that ruleth his own spirit is stronger than he that can take a walled city." (Proverbs 16:32) "And the spirits of the prophets are subject to the prophets." (I Corinthians 14:32.)

2. IMMEDIATE OR QUICK REPENTANCE. Insist that the child apologize to all parties affected, including the Lord.

9. RESISTANCE RESISTED

It is important to train the child to know that if he resists or fights the discipline process, that the discipline will be more severe. My mother would make us go get our own switch off the tree, and if we got one that was too flimsy, she would wear that one out on us and then make us fetch another! We must teach the child to co-operate in this discipline process. If he is allowed to struggle, kick and fight, some one, especially the child, could be injured in his twisting, etc.

10. CRY BABY

Tears of tenderness, love, joy and repentance all have healing qualities, but self pity, crocodile tears, and tears of rage all fit into the category of activity that should not be allowed. What is the saying? "Always childlike, never childish."

11. BEGIN EARLY

A mother asked us once, "How old should my child be before I start to discipline him?" I asked, "How old is your child?" "Three and a half years", she replied. I said, "You've already waited three years too long!" NOTICE! We are NOT advocating that you beat on your baby with anything. But there are many faces of discipline. Look at how many the Good Lord uses on you!

Are you aware of the fact that Indians trained their babies to not cry on command? Sometimes the survival of the entire village depended on it.

During a recent Israeli rescue, I'm told that the commandos jumped into the room where the hostages were held, shouted "EVERY BODY ON THE FLOOR!", and immediately began shooting at everything still standing.

Suppose your baby has been bathed, burped, blessed, bounced and breast-fed. Suppose babykins has been changed, medically examined, rocked, rolled, held, pampered, kissed and "lackasipped". You've smiled at him, checked for clothes too tight, too little or too much. You have checked to see there are no pins sticking and for every other thing you can think of, and you KNOW that it is time for the 'ittle tykiekins' nappypie. Now, at long last, the mother can get some much needed rest as well. This time, HER survival depends on it!

But suppose the little darling has other plans. Suppose bittie itchykins has decided in its cute little head, "I think I'll lay here and yell for a while, just for fun, until mommie picks me up. I would much rather be back in my mommie's arms, nursing contentedly at her breast, or at least lack-a-sipping. For I have decided that I would rather be "gootchy- gooed" than lay here bored and go to sleep. So, I just think I'll lay here and kick and scream and holler and fuss and yell and double up my fists and contort my face and crocodile tear until I get my blessed way by mommie.

Sometimes mom must let baby cry until baby decides that mommie is the mother and that babie is the baby. Baby needs to know that baby's expletives and fist clenching ain't going to get it when it's definitely nap time, and when baby is definitely otherwise o.k.

12. NEVER LET THE CHILD WIN

If you give in at this point, you lose, and the baby loses. You have just trained your child that the madder he gets, the quicker he gets mad, the more he screams, kicks, fusses, contorts, crazies, and crocodiles, then he'll get his way. If a 5 year old does the same thing, and you let him win, (you did before),

111

then everybody loses, including the child. But if you decide that something is definitely the right course for your younger child, and you stand your ground and win, then everyone wins, including the child.

13. LET THE CHILD WIN

Then, there are other times for the child's growth and development, when it is increasingly important to help the child take part in the decision making process. From BEFORE the time they were born, we spoke to and related to our children as though they, (their spirit) could understand. When John the Baptist was a 6 month old "fetus" in the womb of Elizabeth, he KNEW when Mary, newly pregnant with the Christ, entered the room, and he leaped in his mother's womb with JOY! He reacted emotionally in the womb, to something that took place clear across the room!!! (Baby murderers, take notice!) We also related to our children, even when they were babies, as though they could understand, because they could!

14. DON'T KILL OR CRIPPLE THE CHILD'S SPIRIT

In Colossians 3 and Ephesians 6, an interesting thought is presented, (aren't they all!) "Fathers, provoke not your children to anger, LEST THEY BE DISCOURAGED." In all of this, we believe that it is a good thing for a child to have a strong spirit, just so that strong spirit is disciplined and channeled to the fulfillment of the will and purpose and destiny of Almighty God!!! (See our 'Four Horses Vision' in our book, *The Cult Of Cannibals,* available from K.O.G., P.O.7123, Minneapolis, MN., 55407.

15. ALWAYS MINISTER LOVE
AFTER DISCIPLINE

The child needs to be assured of your love and forgiveness after you have disciplined him and he has repented and his spirit is tender. This conveys to him that you have no resentment and that your love for him is not dependent upon his right behavior. Your forgiveness is to be a reflection of the Lord's with us, when we repent. In this way there is to be nothing between you and your child even to the thickness of a cobweb. This is a good policy to follow with others also, as much as is possible.

16. INNOCENT UNTIL PROVEN GUILTY

This policy in our legal system has allowed the guilty to sometimes not be punished, but the policy's purpose is served in its desire to protect the innocent. It insures that the innocent will not be punished. A man of God once said, "I would rather err 999 times in a thousand, in wrongly assuming the best about a person or situation, than to "judge with unrighteous judgement" one time in a thousand." It is of Great importance that you know the facts before you draw your conclusions. I Corinthians 13, the Love Chapter says, "Love always believes the best." How often we see this policy broken - and we see also the broken hearts and friendships that follow.

113

17. LYING - THE "WORST" SIN

There is a lie around that says that all sins are equal. Not so. For example, the sin of blaspheming the Holy Spirit, Jesus said, will never be forgiven, now, or ever. This is when one attributes to satan the works of God - "That's of the devil." Because a relationship of complete trust is so vital, we recommend that you teach your child to see that lying is a most hideous sin, and one that could surely send them smack to hell! God says in Revelation, "...All liars shall have their part in the lake which burneth with fire and brimstone: which is the second death."! We have always taught the children that the punishment for lying will definitely be MORE severe and is an entirely separate offense. Let's say, for example, that the child disobeyed his way into the cookie jar and then lied about it. He is to know that there have been two separate problems-lying and disobedience. He will be talked to about both and punished for each, and more severely so for lying. If you have not obtained or maintained a relationship of trust with the child - then you have no positive or meaningful relationship.

18. DYNAMIC DIALOGUE

It is important to keep the lines of communication open between you and your child at all times, and not only during the discipline process. But it is especially important at that time, also - before, during, and following the discipline. For example, before discipline, it is good to find out the facts, then to explain to the child exactly why he is being punished. Afterward, as we have mentioned, it is good to have an open flow of fellowship, not allowing for pouting, resentment, withdrawal, the silent treatment, etc.

19. REPENT TO THE CHILD
IF YOU ARE WRONG

Although this point should be obvious, it is amazing how often it is not followed, through arrogance, ignorance or "image saving" on the part of the parent. Sometimes the parent thinks that if they apologize to the child, that the child will cease to respect the parent and that the parent's position of authority will be weakened. But just the opposite is true, and the child will greatly respect the honesty and humility in the parent.

20. "PUNITIVE THERAPY"

There is a great deception that exists in the areas of counselling, sociology, and psychology today, and in the penal system generally. This deception is especially evident in the treatment of children. They have come to believe the lie that there is no such thing as "punitive therapy" or "therapeutic punishment". This wrong thinking among these "professionals" is as amazing as the story of "The King Who Had No Clothes!" Do you remember how it goes? A shyster salesman came to town and told the king that he had a special suit of clothes or material that was unique in that only people who were wise and worthy could see it, whereas those who were stupid and unworthy could not. Holding up the "material", the salesman would exclaim, "Isn't this material 'Absotivly' the most beautiful material you ever did see?" Everyone went along with the line because they "didn't want to appear to be ignorant". The day for the great parade came when the king was to show off his new "suit", and the truth was finally brought out in the middle of the parade, by a child who cared more for the "bare facts" than for image dressing.

But the same thing is true among professional counsellors. They don't seem to be able to comprehend that PUNISHMENT HAS TREMEN-DOUSLY EFFECTIVE THERAPEUTIC VALUE. And no where is this more true than in the treatment of children. And no one knows the "bare facts" more than the children, in this regard. They think that the juvenile penal system is a joke. And truth to tell, in many ways and especially with regard to this point, it IS a joke. But it's not funny. The Word of God is so clear on this point as well, as we have seen before: "Foolishness is bound in the heart of a child; but the rod of correction, (a flexible switch), shall drive it far from him." Proverbs 23:15.

21. SPIRITUAL MINISTRY

There is a sense in which every parent is a priest. The Old Testament makes this so clear, as does the New. "But ye are a chosen generation, A ROYAL PRIESTHOOD,...that ye should shew forth the praises of Him who hath called you out of darkness into His marvelous light:" I Peter 2. And from the Book of Revelation, "...Unto Him that loved us, and

116

washed us from our sins in His own blood, and HATH MADE US KINGS AND PRIESTS UNTO GOD AND HIS FATHER: to Him be Glory and dominion for ever and ever. Amen." (From chapter 1).

All through the Scriptures, God has indicated His intent that YOU as the parent should be the child's 'priest' before any other, and that YOU must have the greatest spiritual influence in your child's life!

22. LAYING ON OF HANDS

This is especially important in the area of the "laying on of your hands". Now we are not talking here about spanking. In fact, this is one reason why we recommend the use of the flexible green switch, since God has given your hands such power to bless. Isaac laid his hands on Jacob in Genesis 27. Jacob laid his hands on the sons of Joseph, his grandsons, in Genesis 48. Other examples are given, as well, in Num.8:10; Acts 6:6; 13:3; I Tim.4:14; and in many other places. We are encouraging you that it is your right, as the child's parent, and your responsibility to lay hands regularly upon your child and believe for Christ Himself to bless your child through your hands. How even much more significant it is than even a good night kiss, although the two are not mutually exclusive.

Look at this. After you have been born again by asking Christ into your life as your Savior, Lord and Life, and have turned everything over to Him, having confessed your sins to the Lord and received His forgiveness; if Christ IS your Life, and your hands have been given to the Lord, then YOU CAN BELIEVE FOR YOUR HANDS TO BE THE HANDS OF CHRIST AS HE MINISTERS TO YOUR SPOUSE AND YOUR CHILD THROUGH YOU!!! (and through them, to you!)

One of the fondest memories I have is of our children coming to us on their own volition before they would go to bed insisting, "Would you please bless me!" Then our prayer would go something like this: "Lord, we bless Joey, give him a good night's sleep, bless him Lord, fill him with the Holy Spirit, and help him Lord. Encourage him, and make him to be that mighty man of God that You have called him to be. We impart Your peace, Your protection, Your angels to guard, against bad dreams,......In Jesus' Name, Amen!" Then came the smile, the hug, the good-night kiss and off to bed they would scamper! (Other times, we would bless them after they were already in bed.)

Incidentally, God has given to you who have a spouse the same privilege! Try it, you'll like it.

23. "WHY PRAY, WHEN YOU CAN WORRY" or THE FAMILY ALTAR

How important it is for you to regularly have a "family altar"! A great man of God has said, and it is true, that THE SIMPLEST FORM OF THE CHURCH IS THE FAMILY! We have had some of our greatest church services in the home! One of God's recipes for a service like this is found in I Corinthians 14:26. In our family, or sometimes we gather with another family or two or three or more, (plus some sanctified singles). By the time each of our four children, my wife or perhaps Wells and Sandra and their Josh 'n Andy have shared a verse each, a prayer each, a prophecy each, an original Psalm each, a vision each, a "sharsies" each, from what they have adventured in their exciting walk with God during the week- - - WE HAVE HAD A FULLLL AND SANCTIFIED CHURCH SERVICE that is every bit as pleasing to God if not more so than any "formal church service" in the world!!!

Understand, we are not "hung up" on the necessity of having church in the home, though most of the early New Testament believers had their churches in homes, but we are convinced of the necessity of you and your family having times of definite spiritual sharing and ministering with each other as a family. In fact, we believe that the kind of meeting we have described from I Cor.14:26 must be available to every believer. It should be a small enough group so that everyone has an opportunity to share. Most Christians just sit in their own "pew" and are like the Dead Sea that only takes in but doesn't give out. Your spiritual survival depends upon your having, and taking advantage of, opportunities to minister! If your "church" refuses to give you such opportunity, then we recommend that you join (or start) a church that will! Pastors, note: The largest church in the world is that of Dr. Paul Cho of Korea, who pastors a Pentecostal church. In his church, which has a weekly attendance of over 500,000, he also makes available small weekly "cell" meetings such as the one we describe in the above paragraphs. His book, *The Fourth Dimension*, is available through any good Christian book store, along with others he has written.

But did you know that it is against the law, in some places in the United States for people to have church meetings in their homes? In the mighty Name of Yahweh, we command this situation to be reversed!

24. RAISE THEM TO BE PROPHETS or IS THE HOME A 'NON-PROPHET ORGANIZATION?

Moses said, "I would that all of God's people were prophets." Numbers 11:29. We are defining a prophet here as "someone God considers reliable or faithful enough to consistently talk through." This, of course necessitates your knowing the Lord's voice, and knowing the Lord well enough to raise your children to also be channels of His will. We hereby commission you to raise all of your children to be prophets! Some body may be saying that prophets don't exist today. But that's exactly why we are encouraging you to grow some! What, do you think there's not a need for prophets in the earth today? Don't kid me, 'cauz it's not even funny.

25. TEACH THEM SPIRITUAL WARFARE

One night when our Joshua was about 4 years old, we sent him into the other room to get something. It was dark there in the den, as the light had been turned off. Here came Josh, with wonder on his face, and he exclaimed, "Hey Mom, I can't go in there." I said, even though I'm not Mom, "Why can't you go in there?" He said, "Cauz' there's a Holy Ghost in there!!!" I said, "Well, praise God it was a Holy Ghost!"

On still another night, (we had just moved into this big old house), I sent Joshua up to bed, no problems, it was his bed time, but he was upstairs all by himself. Pretty soon, here he comes, with wonder in his voice, "Hey Mom, (I don't know why he went to Mom at a time like that, but anyway, he says,) "Hey Mom, I can't go up there!" I said, "Why not?" He said, "Cause there's a MONSTER up there!" I gave him instructions, "Joshua, I'll tell you what. You just go back up stairs, and you tell that monster to get out of there in the Mighty Name of Jesus!" So , with a determined demeanor, Joshua (four years old), marches back upstairs, four darkened bedrooms and a bath up there in this new old house, and I heard Josh yell, "MONSTER, YOU GET OUTTA HERE, IN JESUS' NAME!!!" All was silent, so I decided I'd better check on the poor little guy to see if the monster got him. So I hollered up the stairs, "Hey Josh, is everything all right?" He said, from his bed, "Yeah Dad, everything's all right." And everything was all right!

You see, we never taught the children that there is no such thing as ghosts, monsters, goblins, or witches. We just taught them what to do if they ever ran up against one. When I hear about demons or devils, I think and say, "To hell with them." They have a special place prepared for them, and I'm voting that they go there sooner, than later.

Therefore, it is necessary that we teach the children how to walk with God. A friend of ours was nearly raped, but when the attempt was made, she just started speaking in tongues. The man fled in terror. Oh you don't believe in tongues? Well, I'd say that you probably don't know all there is to know about God yet. But then again, neither do I. It worked for her though didn't it?

26. THE FAMILY THAT PLAYS TOGETHER STAYS TOGETHER

Suffice it to say that it is of critical importance that you spend quality time re - creating with your child, (and with your spouse if you are not a single parent). I try to have regular "dates" on an individual basis with each of the children, and my wife, one to one. The Lord says to us in I Timothy 5:8, that we are responsible to meet the family's needs or we have "denied the faith" and are "worse than an infidel." But this meeting of "needs" also applies to recreational, spiritual emotional, friendship-fellowship aspects of the family, not just the financial needs.

27. PRIVATES ARE PRIVATE

Nearly everywhere we tell the story of "Little Orphan Audrey", a much abused friend of ours who lived "happily ever after", we have dear ones coming to us for mental and emotional healing. Child abuse and sexual molesting and incest has reached epidemic proportions in this country. We have two other friends who were raped by their holiness preacher fathers. We have begun to see terrible judgement happening to these parents on the one hand and are seeing beautiful healing and deliverance happening to these children on the other.

The point that we want to make here is that we must respect the children's privacy, and we must teach them to respect ours also. We must not only teach them modesty, but this respect should extend to their rooms, their drawers, their mail, their time, and their bodies, etc.

We are not saying that they should be taught to have wrong fears and hang ups, but about a godly healthy respect for each other that will continue healthy right on into adult living. Of the multitude of mental and emotional hurts, none are so terrifying, damaging or long lasting as incest and sexual abuse. Thank God for His healing delivering Mighty power for His ability to restore and make whole again.

Once again, we declare the terrifying God awful judgement of God on those parents or relatives who rape and incestualize their family members, and on the other hand declare that there is total deliverance and healing for those so victimized.

28. FAMILY MEETINGS

Someone has said that communication dispels deception. But family meetings are such a fabulous opportunity to keep up to date with what's happening in the family. We encourage the children to keep "current" with each other. By this we mean to teach them to keep short accounts, not only with the Lord, but with each other. As the Scriptures say, "Do not let the sun go down on your wrath." Eph.4:26 and again in I John 1:7, "But if we walk in the light, as He is in the light, we have fellowship with one another, and the blood of Jesus Christ...cleanses us from ALL sin!" So it is very important to not allow any thing to come between us in the family - and in God's family too, nothing to come between us even to the thickness of a cob-web. Yet, we know of families that have things accumulate between them of hurts and resentments of a life time long-standing! God tells us to not even let them stand 'til sundown!!! Again, we have the promise that God will NOT forgive us if we don't forgive our fellows. (Matthew 6.)

29. THE FAMILY THAT WORKS TOGETHER STAYS TOGETHER

The Bible has a great deal to say about the subject of work. In the Concordance, one may look under the topic of labor, slothful, lazy, and, of course, work! We advise against the policy of "paying" or bribing the child to do work around the house that is his or her responsibility to perform anyway as a member of the family. This practice could easily develop into a habit, where the child comes to demand payment for basic responsibility. On the other hand, the child gets to share in the blessings that come to the family. Sometimes the child will say, "Aw, that's woman's work." The reply must be given that the family functions as a team and that every one shares in the work responsibilities. The Bible says, "If a person doesn't work, then don't let him eat.!" II Th.3:10-12.

We also lovingly recommend an excellent handout supplement entitled "Under Loving Command" written by Al and Pat Fabrizio. If you are interested in copies of this mini-booklet you can write to us.

REVIEW QUESTIONS — CHAPTER 7

1. What do we mean, "Why pray when you can worry"?

2. Why only say "no" one time?

3. Why NOT put things out of reach, (Except for really dangerous things)?

4. What Book of the Bible is especially filled with Wisdom about raising kids?

5. What do we mean, either kind of abuse?

6. Quote or paraphrase at least 4 verses on child discipline.

7. Why is a flexible green switch better?

8. Why not raise your voice?

9. What do we mean, "Discipline to the point of repentance."

10. What two things are you training the child to do when you discipline to the point of repentance?

11. How many "thwaks" with the switch are recommended at one time before "thwaking" them again?

12. What can one do if the child resists or fights discipline?

13. Are tears always good? Please explain.

14. Approximately when should the discipline of a child begin?

15. What do we mean, "Don't let the child win"?

16. What do we mean, "Let the child win"?

17. Why minister love after discipline?

18. Explain: "nothing between even to the thickness of a cob web?

19. Why have we said that "lying is the worst sin"?

20. Why is "punitive therapy" similar to the king's clothes?

21. What do we mean, "The laying on of hands"?

22. The simplest form of the church is the _____.

23. What should your child do if it ever sees a monster?

24. What do we mean, "Have a 'date' with your kid"?

25. What do we mean, "Keep short accounts"?

8

THE PENTECOSTAL FETUS
or
BABY MURDER!!!

Before we begin this chapter, I want to make something abundantly clear. If you ever feel guilty about something, the solution in God is to admit your guilt, NOT hide it or make an excuse for it; NOT pretend you did no wrong, but to bring it timidly-tenderly before the Lord God Of The Universe and here receive His forgiveness. The psychologist, psychopath, "Christian" scientist", and playboy are WRONG when they tell you to pretend that you did not sin. They are asking you to throw a filthy blanket over something rotten that will be displayed before all at the Judgement Seat Of Christ on that Great Day -UNLESS you ask for and receive God's forgiveness. It is also absolutely necessary that you humbly INVITE Jesus Christ to come in to your heart and life to cleanse you and take over your life completely as Savior, Lord and LIFE!!!!!!!

God can forgive murder. But please make note of this Kingdom principle: IT IS IMPOSSIBLE FOR GOD TO FORGIVE WHAT WE ARE EXCUSING, COVERING OR JUSTIFYING!

I believe that the word "abortion" should be deleted from our vocabulary. It would be like allowing ourselves to change the word "rape" to "Interrupt". The newspapers would say, "The man 'interrupted' her." Some folks are in favor of baby murder. Others like the idea of murdering an unborn baby. Some like to get $$ for murdering babies, while they are still in their mother. But what does God say about it?

Bible Verses For The Baby - Murder

"Then the Word of the Lord came unto me, saying, 'Before I formed thee in the belly I knew thee; and before thou camest forth out of the womb I sanctified thee, and I ordained thee a prophet unto the nations.'" Jeremiah 1:4 & 5. What if he had been "aborted"? What if you had been? Or your mother? Or your spouse? Or your child?

"...Thou hast covered me in my mother's womb. I will praise Thee; for I am fearfully and wonderfully made: marvelous are Thy works; and that my soul knoweth right well. My substance was not hid from Thee, when I was made in secret, and curiously wrought in the lowest parts of the earth. Thine eyes didst see my substance, yet being unperfect; and in Thy Book all my members were written, which in continuance were fashioned when as yet there was none of them." Psalm 139.

"And thou shalt have joy and gladness: and many shall rejoice at his birth. For he shall be great in the sight of the Lord, and shall drink neither wine nor strong drink: and he shall be filled with the Holy Ghost, even from his mother's womb." (An angel to the parents of John the Baptist.) Chapter 1 of St. Luke. Notice in verse 44, "For, lo, as soon as the voice of thy salutation sounded in mine ears, the babe leaped in my womb for joy!!!" What happened here is this, (it makes interesting reading). Mary, just beginning her pregnancy with Christ, comes to see her cousin Elizabeth, who is six months along in her miraculous pregnancy with John the Baptist. And when Mary walks through the door and greets Elizabeth, THE UNBORN "FETUS" OF JOHN THE BAPTIST LEAPS WITH KNOWING RECOGNITION, FROM INSIDE THE WOMB, OF THE NEWLY CREATED "FETUS" OF JESUS CHRIST IN THE WOMB OF MARY FROM CLEAR ACROSS THE ROOM!!!" THE SIX MONTHS OLD "FETUS" ACTUALLY KNEW, AND LEAPED FOR JOY!!! We always related to our unborn children as though they could understand what was happening around them, because - - - they could!!!

A PLACE OF REPENTANCE

"If we confess our sins, He is faithful and just to forgive us our sins, and to cleanse us from ALL unrighteousness!" I John 1:9. Notice here that God promises to take all unrighteousness away, not some, or most, but all!!!

"He that covereth his sins shall not prosper: but whoso confesseth and forsaketh them shall have mercy." Proverbs 28.

"And the times of this ignorance God winked at; but NOW COMMANDETH ALL MEN EVERY WHERE TO REPENT! Because He hath appointed a day in which HE WILL JUDGE THE WORLD IN RIGHTEOUSNESS." Acts 18.

TO THOSE WHO HAVE ABORTED

Please, let me say a gentle word to those of you who have had an abortion and who may have had feelings of guilt from time to time. Let me lovingly say that the Lord wants to put His strong arms around you and give to you of His encouragement, release, forgiveness, strength, healing and comfort.

Please let Him, ask Him, allow Him to do so.

IF AT ANY TIME, DAY OR NIGHT, YOU WOULD LIKE COUNSELLING OR PRAYER ABOUT THIS, OR ANY OTHER MATTER, YOU MAY CALL ON A 24 HOUR BASIS # 612-379-1199. You will be reaching Love Lines, which is an extension of the 700 Club. I was a counsellor with them for over three years, and I am recommending them without a whisper of hesitation. (By the way they need volunteer counsellors, also. And they will even train you for instant ministry!)

OUR EARLY DAYS

When we were carrying each of our babies in the womb, we always acted as though the little bitsy baby in the womb knew what was happening in the immediate vicinity. We acted as though the unborn "fetus" could be affected if we had a wrong attitude towards each other, etc. We blessed and spoke creatively and laid hands on the unborn child, and prayed that God would work some more miracles and bring forth something truly wonderful, carefully nurtured and fashioned in the womb—-by God Himself! And so He did. I hope you have the privilege of meeting the children. You don't have to line up and pay admission to see them. But they are worth it! All praise be to God!

Karen and I earnestly prayed that just the right sperm cell would be joined with exactly the right egg cell and the joining of exactly the right chromosomes chosen by the Lord and that the tiny "embryo" would be filled with the Holy Spirit from the very beginning! Karen and I had both accepted Christ into our lives at an early age and had given ourselves completely to Him. All throughout the pregnancy, we prayed and lived godly lives, going often to fellowship and we remember how the babies would leap and kick within the womb during those times of high praise. The worship would go higher and higher until the very atmosphere was literally charged with the Presence and Glory of God!!! This is what the Bible means by "a godly seed".

I was present at all of the births, as part of the birth team at my wife's side, to encourage, and pray, and bless, and serve and kiss and love and coach her in her breathing during contractions and her relaxation in between. We have all of the births on cassette tape; our laughter and love and joy and triumph. Hey Rocky and Ravolta, eat your heart out, cauz' you ain' got nothin' on me!! Out of gratitude to God, we get up to do a dance for joy before the Lord, and a call to Karen for a date before I come back to the writing!

REVIEW QUESTIONS — CHAPTER 8

1. What is the best solution for guilty feelings?

2. Can God forgive murder?

3. Can you cite an instance in the Bible when a "fetus" reacted with strong positive emotion, when he knew what was happening clear across the room?

4. How much unrighteousness will God take away from us if we confess our sin, and turn away from it?

5. Give here a phone # that you can call for help about any counselling problem, day or night.

6. What in Scriptures is meant by a "godly seed"?

9

THE REBELLIOUS CHILD
or
WHEN YOUR CHILD REBELS

If your child grew up to be too set in his or her rebellious ways before you learned how to properly raise them, there may be times when the child determines absolutely, that it is going to be rebellious, and stay rebellious, no matter what you or God or anyone else does. If the aforementioned keys are unavailing, then there is always the matter of "spiritual quarantine". The child is to know that your home is the property of the Lord Jesus Christ, and that every thing that goes on within it must be according to His Rulership. This Lordship includes, his room, his junk, his behavior, his life. If he refuses to cooperate, then he can be turned over to the correctional authorities as an "incorrigible child". If the child wants to be rebellious, then your umbrella can be gently removed from over his head. Perhaps he will be clever enough to make it in a foster home or in juvenile hall, or ultimately in prison or even at the last, hell itself. But from hell, unfortunately, there is no graduation.

We now include an article that we have written on the subject of "Quarantine" that includes a discussion on discipline, tough love, and sympathy.

SCRIPTURAL DISCIPLINE or SPIRITUAL QUARANTINE

What should a pastor or church do if a member continues to commit adultery, gossip, or drunkenness, etc. and refuses to repent or be delivered from it?

We refuse to give our own opinion or answer to this question! Instead, we turn to the Bible to get God's answer. What does the Bible, the Word of God, say in this situation? Does God ever tell the leaders or the Church to practice spiritual and Scriptural "quarantine"?

The Webster's Dictionary defines quarantine as: "...any isolation imposed to keep contagious diseases, etc. from spreading," or "a place for such isolation."

Ministers of the Gospel frequently have their greatest difficulties and problems over the matter of spiritual discipline. But some of their greatest problems would be solved if they would practice God's instructions for Scriptural or Spiritual "Quarantine".

BIBLE VERSES

Here are some Scriptures that deal with the subject: PLEASE LOOK EACH OF THEM UP, AND MAKE A STUDY OF THEM, (especially, before you would criticize this presentation).

Matthew 10:12-15 (Shake the dust)

Matthew 18:15-18 (Go, then 2-3, then the body, then...)

Matthew 21:12 & Mark 11:15 (Jesus and the money changers)

Luke 17:3 ("If your brother offends you, rebuke him.")

John 20:23 (One's sins are retained if you retain them.)

Acts 5:1-14(Ananias & Sapphira)

Acts 13:6-13 (Bar-Jesus the false prophet)

I Corinthians 5, (Whole chapter)

I Corinthians 6, esp. verses 9,10

Galatians 1:6-12

Galatians 5:14-6:1

I Timothy 5:1,20

I Timothy 6:3-6

II Timothy 3

Titus 1:10-13

Titus 3:10

John 1:9-11

Jude

Revelation 11:3-13

POOR LITTLE SUZIE

Would you think it unkind of parents of a pretty little girl named Suzie to put her in a room by herself, away from the rest of the children, and for them not to allow the rest of the children to play with her? Oh, I forgot to mention that dear little Suzie has come down with a hideously contaminating disease that the others are sure to catch if they have "unquaratined" contact with her! Some uninformed onlooker might sympathetically conclude that the parents are being very very mean and cruel to isolate poor little Suzie this way.

INEXTRICABLE INTERMINGLING

Some years ago, while ministering at a church, a young man came up and asked, "Could you break my bonds?" I said, "What do you mean?" He said, "Y'know, my physical bonds." He said, "Well, me and my girl friend, we been sorta like messin' around y'know." I said, "You mean you and she have been having intercourse?" He said, "Yeah, I mean, right, and now I'd like for you to break my bonds." I thought for a minute, and then replied, "I'll tell you what. Bring me a half a glass of water, and a half glass of milk. If you can pour them together and then separate them back to their original unmixed condition, I'll 'break your bonds' ".

2 (or) 3 POINTS OF VIEW

The play boy says, "It's like shaking hands. That's all there is to it. Afterwards, each goes their separate way, and that's it." And the whore's attitude is not much different from this viewpoint, "Such is the way of an adulterous woman; she eateth, and wipeth her mouth, and saith, I have done no wickedness." Proverbs 30:20.

But God's point of view is what counts, no matter how far-fetched it seems to be, and as you might expect, it is different from the playboy or the mouth-wiping prostitute. God says that when people have sexual intercourse, they become totally inextricably intermingled, body, soul and spirit, as when one pours two containers of liquid together in such a way that one can never unmix them, (inextricable intermingling).

It is our understanding that the Hebrew word for "rib" can also be equally translated "side". With this in mind, consider the following selection from Genesis 2. "But for Adam there was not found an help meet for him. And the Lord God caused a deep sleep to fall upon Adam, and he slept: and He took one of his ribs (or sides), and closed up the flesh instead thereof; and the rib (or side), which the Lord God had taken from man, made He a woman, and brought her unto the man. And Adam said, 'This is now bone of my bones, and flesh of my flesh: she shall be called Woman, because she was taken out of man.' Therefore shall a man leave his father and his mother, and shall cleave unto his wife: and they shall be one flesh (or nature). And they were both naked, the man and his wife, and were not ashamed." (verses 20b-25).

We have a theory, that we of course do not teach as fact, but as a possibility. There is the possibility that the original Adam that God created was so perfect, that Adam had the ability to reproduce without the need for an outside entity, that is, being asexually reproductive, but that there was a problem with loneliness, not being able to fellowship with any except himself, so God put Adam to sleep and took out of him his "female side", closed up his side and

138

made a new creation called a woman, giving her a distinct body, personality, mind and soul. (Please don't scold me for having a theory, don't feel threatened. I'm not saying this is a fact.) But this next part is not theory; it is a fact that when they came together again sexually that they became totally one once again, body, soul, and spirit!

The Apostle Paul says something interesting here, (doesn't he always). *"Now the body is not for fornication, but for the Lord; and the Lord for the body. Know ye not that your bodies are the members of Christ? Shall I then take the members of Christ, and make them the members of an harlot? God forbid. What? Know ye not that he which is joined to a harlot is one body? 'For two', saith He, 'shall be one flesh (or nature).' But he that is joined unto the Lord is one spirit. Flee fornication. Every sin that a man doeth is without the body; but he that committeth fornication sinneth against his own body. What? Know ye not that your body is the temple of the Holy Ghost which is in you, which ye have of God, and ye are not your own? For ye are bought with a price: therefore glorify God in your body, and in your spirit, which are God's."* I Cor.6:13b,14-20. (The Scriptures use of "fornication" here, clearly agrees with the dictionary definition as: "Sexual intercourse with an unmarried person." But some people are acting irresponsibly when they define fornication to include their favorite list of legalistic hang-ups.)

What we are talking about now is fact, not theory. God is saying here that intercourse sexually is like taking a glass of water and a glass of milk, or whatever, and pouring the two back and forth until they become totally blended, or inextricably intermingled. It's not like "wiping your mouth", and it definitely ain't like shaking hands or clinking glasses! Can you see some of the implications here?

For example, a young virgin who is beautiful and innocent could be compared with a beautiful crystal chalice with pure water. But she commits fornication, that is, she has intercourse sexually with someone she is not married to. Let's say that the fellow involved is a playboy whoremonger. At the time of this particular intercourse, a terrifying and hideous thing takes place that causes a total and inextricable intermingling of their bodies, souls, personalities, spirits. It would be like inextricably intermingling a glass of water with a cess pool of urine, coffee, slime, vomit, venereal pus, milk, or blood. Can you see why God is against a person having sex with anything other than their own spouse? And if she commits adultery or fornication with someone else, the inextricable mix simply gets passed along. Could this phenomenon be a partial explanation why there is so much suicide, mental anguish, schizophrenia, split, dual and multiple personality problems among young high school and college men and women??? I believe that this is so.

But there is a solution to the problem!!! Jesus Christ the Lord of The Universe came to earth to take the penalty and punishment for our sin, so as to provide for our total cleansing, purification, forgiveness, restoration, and renewal! He did this by dying on the cross and "taking the rap" for us! But this forgiveness is not ours unless we accept it and appropriate it for ourselves. And we do this by simply opening the door of our lives wide to God and personally inviting Jesus Christ the Creator King of All the Universe to come in like He promises to do in Revelation 3:20. He says, "Look, I'm standing at the door of your life, and I'm knocking. If you will open the door of your life wide to Me and invite Me to come in to take over completely, I will!!!!!!!!" But when you invite God to come in to your life, Jesus is not interested in coming in as your guest or as a roomer. He wants to come in as your Lord and Master and God. And when He comes in, He makes you perfectly new, and alive, and vibrant and clean and virginal and forgiven. (I Jn.1:9). A beautiful crystal clear chalice of the purest most wonderful water of life overflowing!!! That's what you become!!!

But to complicate the problem still more, suppose the girl mentioned above, comes to the Lord Jesus Christ, becomes one nature with God, is made crystal clear and pure, reads her Bible, walks with God, sings in the choir and then gets seduced by whoremonger playboy? If she allows herself to have sex with this guy, it would be like forcing Christ Jesus her Life, to be raped!!! Hold on here. You hold on. And look at the above quotation taken directly from Scripture!: "Shall I then take the members of Christ and unite them with a prostitute? NEVER!!!" (I Corinthians 6:15, NIV)

141

DANGER - QUARANTINE ! ! !

The contamination becomes so hideously-terrifyingly-nauseatingly critical, that the Apostle Paul says that if you know of a brother or sister in the Church Body of Christ that is a practicing adulterer or fornicator, that is, any one who is having sex with what they are not married to, that we are NOT EVEN to be WITH that person, or to fellowship or eat or worship with such a person but that we are to set such a person out side the Church until there is a witness of full and complete turning away from that hideous kind of sinning!. That person will not only have to repent and turn away from the sin but must also have a deliverance imparted to them in a miracle greater than the miraculous separation of two inextricably intermingled cups of liquid!!! The Lord says this in I Corinthians, chapters 5 and 6, and specifically 5:11, b & d , "You are NOT TO ASSOCIATE WITH any person who is known as a brother and yet is immoral...or a railer or a drunkard...with such a person you must NOT BREAK BREAD." And verse 13b, "Therefore, put away from among yourselves those wicked persons." The Lord makes it very clear here that He is talking about "Christians", and not unbelievers.

GOD AIN'T RELIGIOUS OR LEGALISTICALLY MEAN

We'll talk more about legalism, but can you see the love of God in these things? God here is not just giving us a bunch of "no-no's" just to be mean He wants for His people to be healthy, clean and uncontaminated, crystal clear, white and pure. God really does have our best interest in mind! His command is that we not associate with a so-called brother or sister in Christ who is involved in fornication or drunkenness, etc. He commands this so that we do not become hideously contaminated with the "typhoid Mary" kind of contamination that one becomes contaminated with when they have sex with what they are not married to, or in coming under the influence of alcohol or other drugs.

DRUGS AND THEIR EFFECT ON THE HUMAN SPIRIT

The Greek word for witchcraft in the Bible is "pharmakia", from which we get our words like pharmacy, pharmacist, pharmaceutical, etc. The worship of satan, devils and witchcraft has almost always been accompanied by the use of drugs. And the reason drugs are used is their effect on the human spirit. When one ingests drugs, there takes place a disintegration of the natural protective cover or outer protective layer of the human soul that allows free access to that person's inner being to the negative spirit realm to invade, thus allowing access to oppression, obsession and possession by demons and evil spirits. The disintegration of that protective covering is similar to the effect of hot water poured on a thin sheet of ice or wax, or acid being poured on a thin sheet of metal. The real problem in a burn accident is not so much the burn itself, but that the burn destroys the natural protective layer of the skin, and thus allows access for the free invasion of germs and contamination.

Sometimes the "pink elephants", goblins and monsters that had been considered hallucinations have actually been very real and factual things that have not been present or visible before the ingestion of the drug(s). The bar scene from "Star Wars" pictured a room full of monsters and awful looking creatures and was a pretty good description of the way many bars actually look, if one could "see" in the spirit realm. But to get to the point, if a so-called "Christian" takes these drugs, a terrifying thing takes place because Christ is living within, and the door is thrown open for evil spirits to enter or to negatively affect. And because of our unity in the body of Christ, we are easily blessed or cursed by that which exists in our brother or sister in Christ.

God does not want His dear children to be contaminated by "typhoid disease contaminators", and thus He gives instructions for our immunity by putting the source of contamination IN ISOLATION UNDER QUARANTINE, until the problem is solved. Can you see the incredible implications of this? Now, some few may theologically argue that "Christians cannot be possessed by evil spirits", but to be perfectly pragmatically practical, devils live where they live and your blessed doctrine won't make a blessed bit of difference to them, except to let them keep on doing their damndest, undercover. Another argument is that, whereas the Lord may be inhabiting a person's spirit, that the evil spirits may be oppressing, obsessing, or possessing a person's mind, soul, heart or body. These evil spirits MUST GO when there is total repentance (complete once for all turning away from all sin), and prayer of deliverance by those in the body of Christ who have authority from God, who with the word of authority in Jesus' Name cast them out with a word. (Here we recommend the book by Bill Barr from Oconto Ministries entitled *Counselling With Confidence* and our book on marriage called, *The Sexual Ministry*, available by writing Great Commission Ministries, P.O. Box 7123, Minneapolis, MN., 55407).

THE POSITIVE SIDE - SYNERGISM

But so much for the unpleasant aspects. God really has some beautiful things in mind in commanding us to sexual purity! The Bible talks about the synergistically positive effect two people (who are one in Christ-in the union of marriage) can have in the Kingdom of God!!! "Synergism" is defined by Webster as the "cooperative action of discrete agencies such that the total effect is greater than the sum of the effects taken independently." In other words, one may have two different chemicals that aren't much in themselves alone, but when combined may have incredible and powerful results. So it is also for two people who are one in Christ in the sexual bond in marriage. There takes place the inextricable intermingling synergistically of soul and spirit that produces unbelievablly positive results for

145

the Kingdom of God!!! The Bible tells us how that "one chase a thousand, and two put ten thousand to flight" (Deut.32:30.) Jesus said, "Again I say unto you, That if two of you shall agree on earth as touching any thing that they shall ask, it shall be done for them of My Father which is in heaven." (Matt.18:19).

RESTORATION & HEALING

Please understand that one has nothing personal against the one being "quarantined". But what is the proper course when one repents and wants to be restored? It is entirely inappropriate for others to "remember", when God forgets. And it is wrong for us to consider others as "second class citizens of the Kingdom", whom God has restored and forgiven. There are several Scriptures that deal with this:

In I Corinthians, the Apostle Paul "sets an immoral 'Christian' outside the Body of Christ." But in II Corinthians, Paul encourages them to forgive and restore: *"Sufficient to such a man is this punishment, which was inflicted of many. So that contrariwise ye ought rather to forgive him, and comfort him, lest perhaps such an one be swallowed up with overmuch sorrow. Wherefore I beseech you that ye would confirm your love toward him....To whom ye forgive anything, I forgive also: for if I forgave anything, to whom I forgave it, for your sakes forgave I it in the person of Christ...Now thanks be unto Christ who ALWAYS causes us to triumph in Christ, and maketh manifest the savour of His knowledge by us in EVERY PLACE."* II Corinthians 2:6, 7, 8, 10, 14.

SYMPATHY, or "SYMPATHY"

Suppose that there are three people walking down the street. Let's say that the first one falls down of a heart attack. Then the second person sees what happens and feels such commiserating, empathetic, pitying, compassionate, heart felt sympathy, that he or she goes into hysterics, screams and cries, goes into shock and falls beside the first one in a swoon, unconscious. Then the third person almost gruffly shoulders through the crowd, pushes them back, orders a person to call the ambulance, makes the first victim comfortable, jerks open his tie and shirt, ministers mouth to mouth "rescuperation", and heart massage, sees the ambulance on its way, and then calmly straightens out his own tie and walks on down the street. In all this time, he had no worries, sweat or tears.

Question: In this above example, which of the last two people had the most effective compassion or sympathy or commiseration or empathy or love?

One of the greatest deterrents to seeing people helped, is that kind of sick "sympathy" that is weak kneed, sissyfied, sob sistered, crippling, and ineffective - even contributing to the problem.

There is an interesting Scripture from Proverbs (19:18) that says, "Chasten thy son while there is hope, and let not thy soul spare for his crying." And again in Prov.13:24, "He that spareth his rod, (or flexible whipping switch), hateth his son: but he that loveth him chasteneth him betimes." (Also 22:15; 23:13,14; & 29:15,17.)

"MINISTER TO ME ON MY TERMS!"

There is much pressure usually brought to bear on the counsellor by people who want to be ministered to on their terms. Often, they will not only have their problem seemingly properly defined, but they will insist that they know the solution as well, and they want you to give it to them. The kid who wants lots of candy thinks that his problem is lack of candy and that the solution to his problem is lots of candy, and now! So, the pressure is on. The counsellor must objectively look to the Lord to see just what the problem is in the first place, and what the solution is in the second. If Jesus would have healed Lazarus instead of raising him from the dead, He would have failed to do His Father's will. The family and the disciples thought that the problem was a sick man who simply needed to be healed. But Jesus knew that the sick man needed to die! The pressure was on. His dear friends said, "If You had come, Lazarus would not have died!"

SPIRITUAL PROSTITUTION

If a counsellor yields to the pressure to compromise and conform, and sometimes the pressure is great, then that counsellor is a spiritual prostitute. And spiritual prostitution is the worst prostitution of all. Often the counselee says, "Look, if you don't agree with my definition of the problem and the solution and if you don't give it to me, I'll stop being your friend, or quit the church, or be angry with you, or stop contributing ...." etc.

INFANT EXTORTION

Have you ever heard a 6 months old baby say to himself something like this: "Even though I've been held, bounced, burped, blessed, changed and fed; and even though Mommy laid me down for a nap, I have in fact, decided that my problem is that I need to be held, the solution is for Mom to hold me right now, and I'm going to lay here and scream and fuss and cry and wail and yell and grit my gums and clench my fist and wimper and sob and contort my face until I make everybody so miserable that they'll have absolutely no choice but to pamper me and let me have my way."

But the sad fact is that some people get by with this kind of extortion and blackmail well into adulthood and now must learn that God and His representatives will not yield to these extortion attempts. Counsellors become spiritual prostitutes when they give in to the temptation that says, "I will pay you (in favor, friendship, tithes, etc.), if you give me the satisfaction I crave." One of the most common examples of spiritual prostitution is a religious leader who caters to, favors, or compromises in treatment toward someone who has money or power. And our own "fear of man" can as easily lead us into another kind of spiritual prostitution, any time we find ourselves compromising what we know to be the will of God in order to gain, obtain, retain or maintain favor. A common manipulative tool for a child is to say, or imply, that if you don't let him have his way, that you don't love him or that he WON'T love you. Please, dear one, for God's sake, don't compromise.

The prophets and men and women of God have always faced this pressure. "Give me a word from God that I want you to give to me, that satisfies me, and I won't persecute you." Or even worse, "If you give me a word that I don't like, then I won't like you!"

Therefore, in the same way God does with us, we must always act in one another's BEST interest. We must never minister to any one on their terms, and never on our terms, but always on God's terms.

PHONEY PHONING

Jesus must be Lord of all that we say or think or are or do. Our use of the telephone is an example. A friend called today that owed us some money. I did not have time, nor did I feel the leading to talk to this person, so I gave Joshua the message to give, that I did not have the time to talk. The caller replied to him, "If he doesn't have time to talk, then he can forget his money that I have for him." I told Joshua to say, "O.K., Good-bye!" and hang up. Now you may think that this is cold blooded and cruel. But either you have Jesus Christ as your Lord or you have the telephone as your lord. If Jesus is your Lord, then He decides if, or who, you talk to about what and for how long!!! But you may say, "Yes, but I don't want to offend anyone!" But who would you rather offend, your friend, or your Friend the Lord??? Many people actually choose to offend the Lord than to offend people! Strange, but true! Reminds me of a driver who would rather miss a little doggie, squirrel or kitty cat and hit a tree, and kill their whole family because of a misdirected and sick sense of sympathy. And this is also the case where spiritual and Scriptural quarantine are called for where they would rather expose the family of God and their own family to hideous contamination because they would rather not be mean to a poor little critter.

YOU AIN'T BLED YET!

I have a friend who has a pet little sin or two that he just likes to play with and pamper. But then he gets a guilty conscience. He likes to do his precious sin and love his precious Jesus at the same time, but then he gets upset with ministries because they don't give him the "magic" solution. He dares them to give him the solution, but when they even start to begin to commence to apply "tuff luv" he wails and raves like a cat with its tail in the door. His least favorite Scripture seems to be, "Ye have not yet resisted unto blood, striving against sin." Hebrews 12:4.

When I was in Brazil ministering, I heard a true story about a snake whose bite is so deadly that it usually kills within a few seconds. One day a man was cutting his way through the jungle when one of these vipers bit him in the hand. There was no hesitation whatsoever. No deliberation, no debate, no indecision. His machete sword knife was in his other hand. It was - bite - swing - CHOP!!! Off came his arm! Do you think this was cold-blooded? He had no other choice but to "do or die!" And to die is even more cold blooded. When Jesus says in Mark 9:43, "When thy hand offend thee, cut it off," what He really meant

151

was, that we need to really "get tough" with ourselves and stop doing the offending thing, or else cut off the offending member. But no, we have been babied, pampered, "namby-pambied", "moddy-coddled", weak kneed, sissyfied and spoiled even to the point where we would rather enter hell whole than to enter heaven maimed. How about you? Do you love God and hate sin so much that you would rather die, or at least bleed, than sin?!!.

OLD TESTAMENT EXAMPLES

I know that the Old Testament is old, but it still is an indication to us of what God still thinks of sin. He hasn't changed His mind about its awfulness. He chased Adam from the Garden, cut Cain off from his family, cut man off from the earth, destroyed Sodom & Gomorrah, & the first born in Egypt. Then He killed Nadab & Abihu with fire, Korah with the swallowing up of the earth, the rebellious Israelites with the plague, etc. He honored Phinehas for executing the couple while they were fornicating, Samuel for chopping Agag to pieces, also the priest his concubine, Elijah for calling down fire and Elisha for calling out the bears on the children, and calling up leprosy on Gehazi.

NO JUVENILE DELINQUENCY

Did you know that they had no juvenile delinquency in the Old Testament? God's command to the parents was that if their children insisted on staying rebellious, that the people should stone the children to death!!! Now please understand that we are definitely NOT! advocating this, but we mention this for you to see what God thought (and thinks) of rebellion. And although the remedy is different today, God still hates rebellion as much as He ever did!

NEW TESTAMENT EXAMPLES

Jesus drove out the money changers, Paul struck Elymas blind, Peter saw Ananias & Sapphira drop dead, and the two witnesses killing people with fire out of their mouth. The Book of Revelation sees the judgements of God dropping 100 pound hailstones on peoples's heads, 1/3 & 2/3'rds of the earth's population killed, and blood running as high as the bridle of a horse for a distance of 200 miles!

JESUS IS LORD

The whole key to this, as with everything, is that God has a right to be God! And God is looking for those who will obey Him. We are like concerned relatives who run into the operating room of God when the Great Physician is performing a delicate operation. There are two dangers: the one is to grab God's Hand and say, "Thrust the knife deeper." And the other is to say, "Not so deep, not so deep."

FALSE DOCTRINES

The Church has allowed elaborate false doctrines, from "greasy grace" and "sloppy agape" and infernal security and ultimate reconciliation on the one hand to that legalism and religiosity on the other that has people going to hell for spitting on the side-walk! Some people have God looking at our sins through the blood colored glasses of Jesus (or Mary -take your pick), to the point where He can't even see our sin. This is spastic silliness, because God sees us as we are. If we sin, God knows it and will judge us for it, if we do not repent. And if we repent, God doesn't see it any more cause it "ain't" there any more. For more on this, read our book, *The Cult Of Cannibals,* or *God's Answer To Seduction,* c/o K.O.G., P.O.7123, Minneapolis, MN., 55407.

THE RULE OF A RIGHT SPIRIT

The truth of the matter is that it is both possible AND necessary for us to both do right and to be right with a right spirit. God has made it possible. If you want Scriptures and details on this, study again, the chapter on "The King's Greatest Secret", or, of course, read and believe the Bible's many promises that we can consistently walk pleasing before the Lord with a right heart, in spite of the many doctrinal excuses in the churches to the contrary. "But thanks be to God, which giveth us the victory through our Lord Jesus Christ!!!" (I Corinthians 15:57.)

I'll tell you the truth. (Liars burn in hell, and forever is a long, looong time to burn!) If I could disagree with God about something, (and so far, He has won every argument!), I think that He was too hard on Moses for getting a wrong spirit in the desert when he struck the rock. One little bitty act of disobedience and God disqualified him from entering into the Promised Land. Yet God has a right to be God and He shows us again what He thinks of a wrong spirit. But if ever a man had a right to be wrong, Moses did right then. You may think that YOU have it rough with your little brood! Imagine having 6 million rebellious children to put up with—-for 40 YEARS!!! Talk about a frustrated tour guide in the Holy Land!!

Any time someone has gotten a wrong spirit or attitude, they are wrong. It is possible to be wrong with a right attitude and it is possible to be right with a wrong attitude. But of the two, it is far worse to be right, but with a wrong spirit, because God can make a person right, who has a right heart. Remember that, the next time you are "right".

GOD IS GREAT ENOUGH

The question is not, "Am I great enough to keep a right spirit", but "Is God great enough to enable me to keep a right spirit!" The answer is of course, "I can do ALL things through Christ who strengthens me!" Phil.4:13 and "Thanks be unto God who in Christ ALWAYS causes me triumph!" II Cor.2:14 and "In ALL these things we are MORE THAN conquerors through Christ!!!" Rom.8, etc.! If you are really interested in the Good News of this, please, once again we encourage you to lay hold of the revelation of "The King's Greatest Secret!!!"

155

REVIEW - CHAPTER 9

1. As a last resort, what can a parent do with his uncorrectable, wayward, self destructive, or runaway child?

2. What is meant by "Scriptural spiritual quarantine"?

3. What should a pastor do if a church member Christian refuses to repent of adultery, drunkenness, gossip or drugs?

4. Were Suzie's folks cruel to her?

5. What is meant by "inextricable intermingling"?

6. What is the dictionary definition of "fornication"?

7. What Scripture indicates that for a Christian to commit fornication, is like forcing Christ into a "rape-like" situation?

8. What is the Greek word for "witchcraft" or "sorcery"?

9. Explain what probably happens to a person's spirit at the taking excessively of drugs or alcohol.

10. What does "synergism" mean?

11. What does the phrase mean, "second class citizen of the Kingdom"?

12. Should we remember unforgivingly, when God forgettingly forgives?

13. Which person of the last two, in the illustration, had the most "effective" compassion?

14. What is meant by "ministering to a person on their terms"?

15. What is meant by the phrase, "spiritual prostitution"?

16. Have you ever witnessed an infant's extortion attempt?

17. Is Jesus Christ the Lord of your telephone?

18. Are you willing for Christ be the Lord of your pastor's phone? Your friend's?

19. If you are driving your car, and you have only one of two choices, which would you deliberately hit: a cute little kitten or a tree?

20. Would you rather die, or at least bleed, than to sin?

21. Did they have juvenile delinquency in the Old Testament?

22. Do you think that God still hates sin as much as ever?

23. In the Book of Revelation, what was the highest and farthest that blood will run?

24. In your humble opinion, do you think that God has a right to be God?

25. Do you think God sees our sins if we are Christians?

26. Do you believe that it is possible to consistently keep a right spirit?

27. Which do you think is better: To be right, but with a wrong spirit? Or, To be wrong, but with a right spirit? Why?

28. Quote at least 4 Scriptures that indicate that it IS possible to maintain a right spirit, and to be consistently victorious.

10

UNACTUALIZED POTENTIAL ACTUALIZED ! ! !

Oh how God loves the children! He created them! Remember verses like:

"Let the little children come unto Me, and forbid them not! For of such is the Kingdom of God!" Mt.9:14

"He took the children up in His arms and blessed them!" Mt.9:13

"He that causes one of these little ones to stumble, it would be better if he had a mill stone hung around his neck, and that he be dropped into the deepest part of the sea." Mt.18 (May the child molesters and abusers remember this!)

"Unless a person become as a little child, he cannot enter into The Kingdom Of God!" Mt.18:2

"A little child shall lead them." Is.11:6

"Out of the mouth of babes and sucklings hast Thou ordained strength!" Ps.8

"If you...know how to give good gifts unto your children, how MUCH MORE shall your Father which is in Heaven give good things to those who ask Him!!!" Mt.7

"Whosoever therefore shall humble himself as this little child, the same is greatest in the Kingdom Of Heaven!!!" Mt.18

"Whoso shall receive one such little child in My Name receiveth Me!" Mt.18

"Take heed that ye despise NOT one of these little ones; for I say unto you, That in Heaven their angels do always behold the face of their Father which is in heaven!" Mt.18

Some people say that there is no guarantee, even if one raises a child properly, that that child will turn out well - BUT God says:

"TRAIN UP A CHILD IN THE WAY
HE SHOULD GO,
AND WHEN HE IS OLD, HE (or SHE)
WILL **NOT** DEPART FROM IT."

Proverbs 22:6.

IS IT POSSIBLE TO "RAISE PERFECT KIDS?

There is a common devil-ISH saying that "nobody's perfect".

When I announced the name of this book at a meeting in Dallas, Texas, a lady became indignant, and started mumbling louder and louder, "It is impossible to raise perfect kids, I oughtta know, cause mine aren't perfect... and his kids ain't perfect either." (She had never met them!) Ha HA! This lady was my friend by the time the meeting was over. Hmmmmmm.

Do You believe that it is possible to raise perfect children?

In The Bible, Jesus says that "ALL things are possible with God"! (Mark 10:27). What are YOU going to believe?

Do You believe that it is possible to raise perfect children?

Jesus says, "With God, all things are possible"! (Matthew 19:26). What are YOU going to believe?

Do You believe that it is possible to raise perfect children?

In The Bible, God says, "In ALL these things, we are MORE than conquerors through Him who loves us"! (Romans 8:37). What are YOU going to believe?

Do You believe that it is possible to raise perfect children?

The Bible says, "Thanks be unto God Who, in Christ ALWAYS causes us to TRIUMPH, and makes manifest the savour of His knowledge by us IN EVERY PLACE"! (II Corinthians 2:14 & 15). What are YOU going to believe?

Do You believe that it is possible to raise perfect children?

The Bible says, "And God is able to make ALL grace ABOUND toward you that you ALWAYS having ALL SUFFICIENCY for ALL things, may ABOUND toward EVERY GOOD WORK"!!! (II Corinthians 9:8). What are YOU going to believe?

Do You believe that it is possible to raise perfect children?

The Bible says, "I can do ALL THINGS through Christ Who strengthens me"!!! (Phil.4:13). What are YOU going to believe?

Do You believe that it is possible to raise perfect children?

The Bible says, "Thanks be unto God Who gives us the Victory, through our Lord Jesus Christ"! (I Corinthians 15:57). What are YOU going to believe?

Do You believe that it is possible to raise perfect children?

Jesus says, "If two of you agree as touching ANYTHING...I WILL do it for you." (John 14:13 & 14!!!) What are YOU going to believe?

Do You believe that it is possible to raise perfect children?

The Bible says, "ALL THINGS are possible to him (or her) that believes."! (Mark 9:23). What are YOU going to believe?

Do You believe that it is possible to raise perfect children?

Jesus says, "WHAT EVER you ask the Father, in My Name, I WILL do it for you." (John 11:22). What are YOU going to believe?

What are YOU going to believe?

REVIEW QUESTIONS - CHAPTER 10

PLEASE GIVE THE BASIC STATEMENT IN THE FOLLOWING SCRIPTURES:

1. Mark 10:27 -

2. Matthew 19:26 -

3. Romans 8:37 -

4. II Corinthians 2:14 & 15 -

5. II Corinthians 9:8 -

6. Phil.4:1 -

7. I Corinthians 15:57 -

8. John 14:13 & 14 -

9. Mark 9:23 -

10. John 11:22 -

Do you believe that it is possible to raise perfect kids?

(A note to the teacher, here, if this is being taught as a class - if the one taking this course cannot confidently answer in the affirmative that, "Yes, it IS possible to raise perfect children, through Christ!" -then the student is to get a failing grade for the course. When the answer becomes right, and the student agrees with God that, "Yes, this too, is possible.", then the student can become the teacher!!!)

11

COUNSEL FOR COUNSELORS

We felt that this book would not be complete without including some "Kingdom Principles of Counseling", as many of the dear ones who read this book will be involved in counseling. These principles are lessons learned over the years, that may save countless hours of counseling, and may even determine the success of the counseling or even of the family, itself.

1. "PRACTICE WHAT YOU PREACH!"

The Bible says that if you can't shepherd your own marriage and family, how do you expect to shepherd those who have them? God insists that we first have our own act together, taking the "beam from our own eye", as it were, before helping counsel others.

2. ALWAYS MINISTER FROM A 'RIGHT SPIRIT' OR HEART ATTITUDE.

Make sure that you, the counselor, have a right heart attitude and a right relationship with God before attempting to counsel with others. It is a Kingdom Principle that THE QUALITY AND CONDITION OF OUR HEART AND SPIRIT IS ALWAYS BEING BROADCAST, AND COMES THROUGH IN EVERY FORM OF MINISTRY.

At the beginning of our pastoral ministry in 1972, when we pioneered and pastored a church in Phoenix for three years, I determined that I would never preach a sermon, sing a psalm or song, counsel with anyone, lay hands on anyone, prophesy or otherwise minister — if I was aware of any wrong relationship with the Lord, or with my wife or children.

As a testimony to the marvelous grace of Yahweh, (He gets all the credit!), I can say that during that entire three year period of time, I never one time failed to do a form of ministry or counseling because of a wrong relationship between me and Yahweh or Karen and the children.

BUT! One time, I came close! It was a Sunday morning, just before church service, and something was wrong between Karen and me. She was upset with me about something, (I forget what the issue was, but I'm sure that it was her fault! Ha HA !) I remember that I pleaded with her, I apologized, I repented, I may have even tried to use my authority as "the husband" or as "the pastor" — but all to no avail. At fifteen minutes before church time, with the problem still unresolved, an idea came to me. I jumped into the car, ran up to the corner drug store, bought some sweets, a "sweet somethings" — "I love you" card, and some "sweet smellums skunk water" type perfume, had it all gift wrapped, and went dashing back to the service, which was already getting underway. All I had time to do, on my way up front, was to lovingly lay all this stuff in my wife's lap. The next time I turned around to look at her, the tears

165

KINGDOM CONTRACT OF TOTAL COMMITMENT TO THE LORD JESUS CHRIST KING OF KINGS AND THE LORD OF LORDS

I hereby totally surrender all that I have and am, or shall ever have or be, completely to Jesus Christ (all other conditions and terms of this contract to be filled in later by the Lord Jesus Christ).

-
-
-
-
-
-
-
-
-
-
-
-
-
-

Date _____

Witness _____ **GOD** _____

Signature _____

of tenderness, were running down her cheeks, and then we lived happily ever after!!! We had church!!!

This is a principle in ministry that I have maintained. Only yesterday, in the church service, I turned the service over to someone else, long enough for me to go back to where my wife and daughters were sitting to make sure that everything was O.K. It was!

Again, if someone asks me, "Are you perfect?" My answer is, "That's what Christ commands!" (Matthew 5:48). If they say, "Don't you ever get a wrong spirit towards your wife?" I reply, "I don't recommend it!" People often want you to admit that you cannot keep a right spirit, in order that they'll have an excuse for their wrong spirit, or heart attitude.

Anyway, the point is, that a right heart attitude and relationship is necessary on the counselor's part, or, that which is in his spirit will be communicated and imparted through his counseling and ministry.

(For more information about this, please see the chapter on "The King's Greatest Secret!")

3. GET THEM TO AGREE THAT JESUS WILL BE LORD!

Before beginning with the counseling itself, and before getting into the "issues", insist that the couple or the child will agree to sign the "Kingdom Contract", or otherwise agree to do what EVER God wants them to do! Otherwise you'll be wasting your time. I have held the door open to the room in which we were counseling, and said, "There are counselors & churches all over town that cater to a "percentage

167

commitment" in discipleship. You are welcome to go to one of them! If you really really want to do the will of God, I am willing to lay down my life for you, but if you want to play games of compromise with God, I don't have time to cross the street for you!" (We are not, of course, talking about sincere seekers.)

Dear ones, we only have time, in this short life, to do the will of God. We are all too busy than to do things outside His Will for us. God's will for us, His Plan for us, His Blueprint, His destiny for us is more than a full time job. None of us is smart, or wise enough or educated enough to be able to counsel people who refuse to agree to the Will of God. If they refuse, then the best thing I can do is wish them, "good-luck", because they'll need all the "luck" they can get, outside of the will of God! God Himself **will** respect their wishes for compromise, will not cross their will, and **will** send them to an eternity in hell, if that's what they chose.

Remember, GOD **WILL** ASSUME 100% RES-PONSIBILITY FOR A LIFE THAT'S TOTALLY COMMITTED TO HIM; He will assume a percentage responsibility for a life that's only partly committed to Him, but He assumes no responsibility whatsoever for a life that refuses or neglects to be committed to Him. He respects and honors our will and choice in the matter.

To spend valuable time trying to patch things up with people who couldn't care less about the will of God is a waste. Therefore, the first part of the counseling time is spent making sure of their commitment to the Perfect Will of God. I personally, refuse to progress beyond this point until I get their agreement, or the agreement of at least one of them, if they are married. If they are contemplating marriage, I recommend that the relationship be broken off, if one of the two is not totally committed to do God's Will. If they are married, I will counsel them if only one of them is willing. The Scripture says, "I will avenge their disobedience, when your obedience is complete." God will use the commitment of either one of them as a "fulcrum" from which to apply leverage to the other towards the Will of God.

4. MAKE IT TOTALLY CLEAR THAT YOU ARE NOT MINISTERING FROM YOUR OWN WISDOM, AND THAT YOU ARE NOT CAPABLE IN YOURSELF TO COUNSEL THEM, BUT ONLY THE LORD THROUGH YOU. (II CORINTHIANS 3:5; JOHN 5:19,30) We must never have self confidence, but God-confidence.

5. MAINTAIN STRICT CONFIDENTIALITY. THIS POINT MUST BE ONE OF THE FIRST, BECAUSE IT IS VERY VERY BASIC TO COUN-SELING. Once, long ago, I was in an elder's meeting where something of the strictest confidentiality was mentioned. We were all sworn to secrecy, by the presiding apostolic ministry, but before that apostle reached home, less than 15 minutes later, his wife had received a phone call from someone else who had received a phone call which included the very information we were supposed to have kept secret. On the other hand, often Karen will tell me something

she finds out in the natural course of events, that I knew about in private counsel perhaps a year before, but did not share with her, because God has taught me the importance of maintaining a "fiduciary" relationship - that is, a relationship of trust. Besides being held responsible before God, to maintain confidence, one is also open to being sued in a court of law for breaking confidence. In addition, people often will not share what they desperately NEED to share, if they do not feel secure.

6. INCLUDE THE LORD IN THE SESSION, TURNING TO HIM OFTEN IN PRAYER. LEARN THE PRACTICE OF INCLUDING GOD IN MANY, MANY CONVERSATIONS. WHEN SOMEONE ASKS ME A QUESTION I DON'T KNOW THE ANSWER TO, OFTEN I WILL, WITHOUT CLOSING MY EYES, TURN TO GOD AND SAY, "FATHER, WHAT ABOUT THIS, PLEASE KEEP ON BEING OUR WISDOM AND OUR MIND."

7. HAVE ALL PARTIES BEING COUNSELED BE PREPARED TO TAKE NOTES.

The reason for this is, that often during a counseling session, a question or comment may come to one or more of the people sitting by, that they may want to ask or share, but they don't want to interrupt the person who needs to complete the expression of their point. They may also want to remember things that are said for future benefit.

8. Remind them that "WE WRESTLE NOT AGAINST FLESH AND BLOOD, but against

principalities and powers, spiritual wickedness in high places,.." etc. We told this story before, but here we tell it again, about a couple who were having an argument. Suddenly, the husband caught the reflection of light from his wife's ring, and "saw the light". He stopped mid-sentence, went around the table to his wife, gently took her in his arms, and said, "Darling, I'm on YOUR side!"

9. ALWAYS REMAIN AS TEACHABLE AS YOU ARE RIGHT NOW!

I was working on construction, and we were doing the concrete work for a garage floor and drive way for an older minister who was just retiring from the ministry. As I was just getting started out in the ministry, I wanted to learn from the old gentleman. I asked him, "Sir, with your experience of years in the ministry, if you had just one word of advice or counsel for a me, young man just starting out in the ministry, what would that advice or counsel be?" After pausing to ponder the question for a moment, he said, "ALWAYS REMAIN AS TEACHABLE AS YOU ARE RIGHT NOW!" I have always tried to keep that advice in mind, and to follow it. For example, if you have advice or counsel or rebukes or criticism that you would like to give to me, I would really appreciate it if you would share it with me. I would rather that you NOT share your negative opinion about me to someone else. It would be difficult for me to learn from your gossip about me. It will be easy for me to learn from what you have to share with me about me. Thank you!

I teach people that we must love correction, if we would be wise. I teach people that we must be able to have an experience where we keep a right heart attitude when the wrong person comes to us at the wrong time with the wrong attitude giving the wrong advice in a wrong manner.

10. IT IS BEST TO NOT COUNSEL ALONE!

The Bible says that "In a multitude of counselors there is safety." There are a number of very good reasons for this:

A. CONFIRMATION - The Bible says, "At the word of two or three witnesses, let every word be established." We are not looking for a "yes man" here, but one who, with integrity, will add confirmation, and thus greater authority to the counsel given."

B. AFFIRMATION - It always amazes me how people being counseled have what is known as "selective hearing", or, even worse, "twisted hearing". We have seen people counseled that have sworn that that the counsel that the counselor gave was one thing, but when we checked with that counselor, he would say, "I never said that at all!!!"

C. AUTHORITY - The Bible says that, "If two of you agree as touching anything, it shall be done." and "One of you will be able to chase a thousand, but two of you will be able to put ten thousand to flight." Thus the available amount of wisdom is increased synergistically, and the authority to bind and loose, and take care of the problem.

D. SEXUAL SAFETY - We are aware of classic situations where someone will wrongly accuse the counselor of sexual harassment, or of other times where the counselor actually did make sexual advances. In still other situations, where the counseling had been perfectly moral, a third suspicious or jealous party, assumed, and then passed along that suspicion, as truth! The Bible says, "Abstain from every appearance of evil." and "Let not your good be evil spoken of." If there is another counselor present, the possibility of these problems is minimized.

E. HUMILITY — When more than one counselor is present, and positive change takes place, it is more difficult for any one individual to take all the credit. This minimizes a "groupie" or "man-worship" or "counselor fixation" tendency. All of the credit for any good belongs to - - - the Lord Yahweh!

KAREN HAS SOME THOUGHTS

Here are some thoughts from Karen, my precious wife: She believes that is is important to teach the couple to remember the following:

11. TEACH THEM TO EXPRESS GRATITUDE AND APPRECIATION FOR EACH OTHER! "To have a time when husband and wife or the family sit down together and share what they love about each other. 'One of the things I love about you is...' Have you ever done this? Then don't knock it!! Oh, how our spirits need edification! Isn't the Word clear on this about how we are to build one another up? What

happens to you when someone comes up to you and says something nice about you? Something takes place inside you! There is a confidence that is built in yourself (in the Lord) because of what the other person has said to you. We already know how to criticize, but have we learned how to edify? See what happens when you spend five minutes telling one another what you love about each other.

12. TEACH THEM TO SEE EACH OTHER FROM GOD'S PERSPECTIVE — SEE EACH OTHER THROUGH EYES OF LOVE AND FAITH! "Another point is to have faith for one another and to see him or her as how God sees them. We build faith in them by our contending for them and believing for them as to what God has said."

13. TEACH THEM THE POWER AND PRIVI-LEGE OF BLESSING! "If you have an unsaved mate and it is difficult to communicate with him, (or her), if your spouse is willing to have sex with you, at this time, his, (or her), heart or spirit will be very open to you! It is at this time that you can really release your faith and blessing. And pray! (Not necessarily out loud because they may not want that.) But God will honor your faith and start working in their lives. And they won't even know what hit them! God has given us power to bless as believers. Now, will He not honor that faith? We can bless their food as we prepare it or bless their shoes before they walk in them all day. We can bless their pillow and believe God to impart to them whatever they need. Let's exercise our faith!!! I remember a friend of mine who was so troubled about

her son not doing well in school academically. So she would go in after he was asleep and pray for him that God would give him wisdom and knowledge. Before long he was getting A's. Jesus commands us to bless and curse not. There is power in blessing!"

14. TEACH AN ATTITUDE OF GRATITUDE! Some folks think that the world owes them a living and that they deserve to be treated well by their spouse and others. It is actually true, that none of us deserve more than an eternity in hell!!! Some husbands, wives or children gripe, grumble and complain, when, in fact, Ephesians 2:8-10 clearly states that none of us deserves other than hell. We could never hope to earn any thing more than hell. Salvation is, pure and plain - a totally undeserved GIFT from God, out of the goodness of His Great God's Heart, and NOT because we earned or deserve it!!! This should cause all of us to stop griping and complaining about life's lowly lot, but to give Yahweh great thanks for each undeserved drop of water, and for every unmerited breath of even smog filled air!!! Even a dandelion looks good, and a little posy looks and smells sweet though none notices or appreciates - simply because, that's what it was created to do!!! And we are created for praise! My friend Ed Hussman points out, "How a blind man would love to see, even a butter-cup or a dandelion! How grateful we should be for our eyes, our ears, our senses!"

If we could only get a "revelation" of this fact that we all deserve nothing more than an eternity in hell!

Do you see it? Once we do, we will be forever deeeeeeeeeeeeeply grateful. So much counsel would be eliminated, so many problems would be solved, (or never arise in the first place), IF only people would be grateful instead of grumpy. So many adults and children have a "style of living, to which they've become accustomed," or a "fantasy ideal in their mind", and when their fantasy doesn't become a reality, they are unhappy and unpleasant. In contrast, is the person who realizes that he or she only deserves the flames of hell, and is incurably and gloriously grateful for the sweet privilege of life itself! What a refreshing joy to be with such as these! What a thrill to be with people like this.

15. TEACH THAT WE CAN AND MUST EXERCISE OUR WILL GOD-WARD

There are a number of situations where it is extremely important to know that we can fulfill the will of God by simply exercising our will God-ward. For example, let's:

16. DEAL WITH THE MYTH OF "FALLING IN LOVE"!

There is a great lie that has been "foisted" upon western civilization that comes out of Babylon and Hollywood, called "falling in love". We have been brainwashed, hypnotized, hoodwinked and mesmerized into thinking that to "fall in love" was God's way - but it ain't! It is because of this lie that some of the dear ones, sometimes even ministers or others in the church, have "messed up" so badly.

When God gives us a command, He expects us to

carry it out whether we "feel" like it or not. This immediately helps us —

17. DEFINE: "FLESHLY", "SOUL-ISH" OR "SPIRITUAL"

A fleshly person does what their flesh and their body, their feelings, lusts, cravings, wants and desires tell them what to do, regardless of what God is telling them. This person is a prisoner or a victim of his own flesh. When the devil jerks or yanks on the ring that's in the nose of their flesh, the person meekly, blindly, suicidally follows along down the slimy, slippery road to a slow but everlasting death!!!

A soul-ish person does what their emotions or their mind tells them to do, regardless of what God is telling them. If the soulish person wakes up in the morning, and their soul tells them to be depressed, they say, "Uh, yah, er, O.K., any thing you say! Jes' make me feel depressed, an' I'll lay in bed all day!" These are also led around by a ring in their nose, as victims of their own fickle, undependable, fluctuating, vacillating, spastic emotions, feelings and thoughts. These pathetic creatures say, "Never mind what God or the Bible says, I FEEL this way, or I THINK that way — therefore...." The "soulishly religious" person, (as opposed to the spiritual person), is also in the soulish category. There are actually "religious", but evil spirits who try to put on a religious front. Remember, both in the Garden and at the Temptation of Christ, the devil quoted Scripture. Insane asylums, typically have a large percentage of people who are "religious".

177

But a spiritual person does what God says, no matter who, how, when, what, why, or where, how much it costs, how inconvenient it is, what they feel like, what they think, what their flesh is screaming for them to do, or how much persecution it results in.

The spiritual person does God's will - PERIOD! "If God says it, that settles it!" The spiritual person knows that ONE MUST NEVER DETERMINE THE WILL OF GOD BY LOOKING AT FEELINGS, FINANCES, OR CIRCUMSTANCES, BUT BY WHAT GOD SAYS!!!

18. PRESENT:

A FORMULA FOR DATING,
or
"MOM'S TALK BY THE STAIRS"

I remember the day, when I was a young teen-ager when my darling mommy and me had a good old heart to heart talk. While she was ironing some clothes, I was sitting on the basement stairs. She said words to this effect, "John, you need to decide whether or not God has called you to walk with Him, to serve Him." (Of course, I knew that He had. I knew that He was calling all of us to walk close to Him.) She continued, "If God has called you to walk with Him, then you need to decide to not let anything interfere with that call! And at the top of that "anything" list, you can put . . . the opposite sex!" She continued, "John, more people fall in love with the wrong person or at the wrong time, and get side-tracked from what God wants them to do, than just about any other thing.

But you've got to make up your mind, if God has called you to walk with Him, to not let ANYTHING or ANYONE distract you from doing the will of God FOR ANY REASON!!!" So, guess what I did. I quietly, simply made up my mind to not allow myself to "fall in love" until God Himself revealed to me that it was God's time and God's choice of a partner for my life!

I WAS GOOD WITH MY HANDS!

In the dating that I did, I determined that I would honor God and that my hands would behave themselves. We prayed on nearly every date. I made for myself what some might call a silly rule, but it accomplished what I intended. I decided that I would not have more than three dates in a row with the same girl, but that if I really liked her, that I would date someone else in between, and then date her again. This policy let both of us know that I was not ready to "get serious". In all of this, I simply refused to allow myself to "fall in love", until I knew that it was God's time and God's choice.

ANCIENT HISTORY

After I graduated from Bethel College, I was led to go to Bethany Fellowship Missionary Training Center. The first week I was there I saw a student that caught my attention. God spoke to me and revealed to me that this was the one that He had chosen for me that would be my wife, but that it still was not the time to become emotionally involved. After 18 whole months had transpired, God instructed me to CHOSE

179

TO LOVE HER, and that it was the time for me to DECLARE MY LOVE to her, and to PLACE MY LOVE UPON her. I can clearly remember the occasion. There, under the cross, on the south side of the chapel building, just as the sun was setting, I took Karen by the hand, and, for the first time in my life, told a woman that I loved her. Then, we lived happily ever after!

DO YOU WANT TO LIVE "HAPPILY EVER AFTER"?

Incidentally, in my walk with God, He had previously taken me through a time when He first asked me if I was willing to be single if He wanted me to. I sincerely thought that by saying
"yes", I would be forever bound to the celibate life —but I said a deeeeeeeeeeeeeeeply sincere "yes" anyhow. Then, God asked me if I would be willing to marry ANY ONE that He chose for me, no matter how ugly or dumb or fat or skinny or old or smelly she was. Thinking that surely God was going to give me the worst, (but having confidence that He was smarter than me, and that He had my best interest in mind), again I said a deeeeeeply sincere "yes" to God. Guess what happened——. God gave me——- the BEST!!! And then we lived happily ever after!!!

SEX EDUCATION

The best way of educating and teaching the children about sexual things is to have a healthy attitude about sexual things yourself. Thus, it is extremely important for you to not be guilty of sexual promiscuity or license on the one hand, nor guilty of prudishness, restraint and hang ups on the other. We wholeheartedly recommend our book, *THE SEXUAL MINISTRY*, in which we help married people to be free of hang ups and restraint, and also to have a healthy righteousness.

Secondly, we have explained to our children that sex is a "do-not-open-before-marriage" kind of package. That is, we encourage that the "seed of sexual awareness and experimentation" be kept "ungerminated" or dormant until marriage. We explain how the whole story of "Pandora's Box" really does apply here, and that all of us should "keep the lid on it" until marriage, at which time it is a "no holds barred" kind of happily ever after gift from God. We teach them "The Sanctity Of Celibacy", and the holy advantage of "keeping one's self pure" until marriage.

Thirdly, we recommend that during the engagement, that extensive pre-marriage counselling take place to insure that the couple will enter fully prepared and commissioned to begin their "Sexual Ministry". That's why we wrote the book, *THE SEXUAL MINISTRY*.

19. NEVER MINISTER TO PEOPLE ON THEIR TERMS, OR ON YOUR TERMS, BUT ONLY ON GOD'S TERMS! One of the greatest temptations in counseling is to minister to people on their terms, or on ours. The pressure is almost always on. People usually have their problem figured out, and often think they know what the solution is. They want you

181

to agree with their definition of both the problem and the solution, want you to help them work out their solution, then they will be happy. In the story of the healing of Lazarus, for example, his friends knew that the simple solution to his problem was for Jesus to heal, when, in fact, it was the perfect will of God that Lazarus die! (By the way, this is the only place indicated in the New Testament, that sickness was God's will!) Jesus would have sinned, if He had healed His friend, when Father wanted him to die. Why? So He could raise Lazarus from the dead!!! But they didn't know that ahead of time! I've seen people get so angry and intimidating when they don't get their way! But let's face it folks, if we yield to the pressure to compromise the will of God for whoever for whatever reason, then we are guilty of spiritual prostitution —the worst kind of prostitution there is!

20. IN THE COUNSELING, GET THEM TO AGREE THAT THEY WILL ACCEPT YOU AS THE REFEREE, AND THEY WILL CO-OPERATE WITH YOU IN THE FLOW OF COUNSELING. SOMEONE MUST LEAD.

In other words, insist that they give to you the power to control the flow of conversation. The counseling must be under the control of the the Holy Spirit. For example, if the husband is doing catharsis, that is, "getting it out of his system", and is sharing needed information, it may be counterproductive for the wife or child to interrupt, or vice versa. On the other hand, one of them may be speaking in a manner that is hurtful, cruel, mean or destructive, to one's self or the other. In this case, the counselor must be in control, and stop the hurt from happening.

21. REMIND THEM THAT THE WITH-HOLDING OF AFFECTION IS CRIMINAL, AND IS DEFINITELY AGAINST THE LAW OF LOVE AND OF THE KINGDOM!

22. EMPHASIZE THE IMPORTANCE OF REPENTANCE. ASK EACH OF THEM TWO QUESTIONS: # 1, "IN THESE PROBLEMS THAT YOU ARE FACING, WHAT PERCENTAGE, 1 TO 100, WOULD YOU SAY THAT YOU ARE TO BLAME, OR ARE PART OF THE PROBLEM; AND # 2, WHAT PERCENTAGE WOULD YOU SAY THAT THE OTHER PERSON IS TO BLAME???

Have them write these answers down on a private piece of paper. Then gently lead them to understand that they would have been safe, in the vast majority of cases if they had assumed 100% of the responsibility for the problem. Repentance is healthy! I remember listening to an elder's wife tell me, for about 45 minutes, all of the things that were the matter with her husband, but nothing about where she was a contributor to the problem. Yet, God was revealing to me that she was the problem, not her husband. So, when she paused for breath, I said to her very gently, "Dear One, I believe that I have a solution to your problem with your husband." She said, "Tell me." I said, "I believe that God has shown me that your problem would be solved, if you would accept 100% of the blame — and repent!" She looked at me like I had given her a sledge hammer blow between her eyes — but to my knowledge, she never did repent, and the problem has continued for more than a dozen years!!! (I would have told him the same!)

23. REMIND THEM THAT GOD COMMANDS THEM TO REPENT AND GRANT FORGIVENESS 70 X 7 IN 1 DAY - EVERY DAY!!!

We invite a curse upon ourselves in the Lord's Prayer — we say, "Lord, please be exactly as forgiving toward me, in my sins against You, as I am in forgiving the sins of others toward me." And then Jesus gave us this promise that should be in all the "promise boxes", (and occasionally , in the fortune cookies), "For if you do not forgive others, for their wrongs done to you, neither will your Heavenly Father forgive you for your sin toward Him!" I have yet to counsel anyone who used up all of their 490 in one day!!!

24. ATTENTION: EVERY COUNSELOR: IT IS OF ABSOLUTE NECESSITY FOR YOU, AND THE PEOPLE YOU ARE COUNSELING TO HAVE A "GUT LEVEL GRASP" - A CLEAR UNDERSTANDING OF: THE KING'S GREATEST SECRET, IF THE COUNSELING IS TO BE TOTALLY SUCCESSFUL. FOR IF YOU KNOW THE "SECRET", THEN IT WILL BE JESUS CHRIST, AND NOT YOU, WHO DOES THE COUNSELING, AND IT WILL BE JESUS CHRIST, THROUGH THEM WHO FULFILLS THE RE-QUIREMENTS OF GOD FOR A PERFECT FAMILY OR MARRIAGE!!! Please, we plead with

you, do not leave any stone unturned, until you come into a deeeeeep and clear understanding of this Greatest all encompassing Secret!!!

25. LET GOD USE YOU IN THE HEALING OF EVERY AREA OF A PERSON'S BODY, SOUL AND SPIRIT: LOVELY, LOVELY HEALING TO EACH PERSON'S HURTING HEART, AND MIND, AND EMOTIONS, AND MEMORIES, AND NERVES, AND DAMAGE FROM PAST SINS AND UNPLEASANT CIRCUMSTANCES, AND RESENTMENTS AND BITTERNESSES AND UNFORGIVENESS.

Very gently lay your hands on the person being prayed for and believe for Jesus Christ your Life to minister whatever He wants to minister to that person through you. You are not sufficient in yourself so as to think anything of yourself, but your "sufficiency is of God, who is able to make you an able minister of the covenant."

26. MINISTER DELIVERANCE IF IT IS NEEDED.

By "deliverance", we mean deliverance from every form of demon oppression, obsession, or possession. There are some Christians who have been FOOLISHLY tricked into believing that a Christian cannot become demon possessed, just as there are some Christians who have been FOOLISHLY tricked into believing that every Christian is filled with God's Holy Spirit, Unfortunately, thus saith the Lord, "neither generalization is true." We:

27. BELIEVE IN "DELIVERANCE BY THE DISPLACEMENT METHOD".

Some "deliverance ministries" see devils behind every bush, whereas other counselors and psychologists think that the only place demons grow is "in Africa some place". They wouldn't recognize a demon if one of them jabbed them with a pitchfork.

Some "deliverance ministries" make the cure seem worse than the cause. I've seen or heard of deliverance sessions where the demons get to show off as a preliminary to the deliverance. It sometimes gets to be a coughing, vomiting, spitting, knock down, drag out, drawn out, spastic affair. I've seen counselors, get their clothes torn and dirty, their watches broken, their skin bitten or scratched. But I believe in what I call "Deliverance By the Displacement Method".

First of all, I assume that NO MATTER HOW POSSESSED A PERSON IS, THEY CAN STILL EXERCISE THEIR WILL FOR DELIVERANCE. IF THEY REFUSE TO FULLY CO-OPERATE IN THE MINISTRY TO THEM, I REFUSE TO MINISTER TO THEM! Let me share with you what I believe to be the Scriptural basis for this assumption. In Mark 5 and in Luke 8, we have the story of the man who had the "legion" of demons. Now, a legion was a Roman troop of 6,000 soldiers. So, let's, for the purpose of discussion, assume that this fellow had 6,000 demons in him! There were 2,000 hogs that were killed, as a result! But, even if we assume that there were only 2,000 demons, not a single solitary one of them wanted the man they possessed to do even one of the first four things that the man did when he saw Jesus. Here the man has, let's say between 2,000 and 6,000 demons in him. But, the first thing that he does, is SEE JESUS! The second thing he does is, RUN TO JESUS! The third thing he does is BOW DOWN TO JESUS, and the fourth thing the demon possessed man does is WORSHIP JESUS!!! By this, I am believing that, no matter how possessed a person is, that if they really desire and are ready for deliverance, that they will co-operate fully in the deliverance process. Jesus did not go around indiscriminately casting out demons, but as the Father led Him, so He did, and as the Father leads us, so must we!

"DISPLACEMENT DELIVERANCE"

Here is how we suggest that a counselor proceed with ministry: 1) If the person has not personally, knowingly INVITED the Lord and Savior JESUS CHRIST TO COME INTO THEIR HEART AND LIFE, then we lead them in this step.

2) If the person has not "SIGNED THE BLANK CONTRACT" and accepted Jesus Christ as the Absolute and Only Lord and Master of their life, then we lead them into a prayer that accomplishes this.

3) We lead the person to understand, "THE KING'S GREATEST SECRET", to realize and reckon themselves to be "crucified, dead and buried with Christ, resurrected, risen, and reigning on the Throne with Christ, and to accept Jesus Christ now to

187

actually BEEEEEEEEEEEE and become that person's LIFE!!!

4) Then, we lead the person to REPENT of every thing in his or her life of which God does not approve. After they "I John 1:9 it", we assure them that they are, as I John 1:9 says, "cleansed from all, (NOT most), unrighteousness."

5) Then we lead them to RECEIVE THE BAPTISM OF THE HOLY SPIRIT, or the Fullness, or the Infilling of the Holy Spirit in All of His Fullness. Since God, in the Bible says that He gives the Holy Spirit to them who ask Him", those who wish to receive the Holy Spirit in His fullness, have only to ask. Meanwhile, if there are those for whom the Baptism of the Holy Spirit is "against their religion", then they don't have to ask, and very simply, they don't have to receive. But, there is a danger here, Jesus pointed out that if the "HOUSE IS NOT FILLED," then the demons can come back 7 times worse than before! The command of the Scripture still is, "BE YE BEING FILLED WITH THE HOLY SPIRIT!" or as the Amplified New Testament says in Ephesians 3:19b, "That ye may be filled through all your being unto ALL THE FULLNESS OF GOD, that is, may have THE RICHEST MEASURE OF THE DIVINE PRESENCE, and become a body WHOLLY FILLED AND FLOODED WITH GOD HIMSELF." Just because you have spoken in tongues, or are a Baptist, doesn't guarantee that you are RIGHT NOW FILLED with the fullness of God. Only the state "being filled with the Holy Spirit" RIGHT NOW,

guarantees that you are "filled with the Holy Spirit right now!!!"

6) Occasionally, there may remain a little "MOPPING UP ACTION" and, just to make sure, you can lead the person in a prayer like this: "Father God, in Jesus' Name, I bind, cast out and off and away from me and this place into the abyss, every principality and power, every spiritual wickedness in high places, every ruler of the darkness of the air. The Lord rebuke you satan, the Lord Jesus rebuke you demons and devils, I bind you and cast you into the holding place of demons awaiting judgement. In Jesus' Name, AMEN!" (SEE NIV BIBLE AND FOOTNOTE AT II PETER 2:4), "...God did not spare angels when they sinned, (demons), but sent them to hell, (Greek word is 'Tartarus'), putting them into gloomy dungeons, (or into chains of darkness), to be held for judgement."

7) TEACH THEM TO READ THE BIBLE THROUGH, CHAPTER BY CHAPTER, WITHOUT SKIPPING ANY PARTS! Have them start with the New Testament, and write that day's date after each chapter, portion or page that they read. The "displacement method" attempts to get the person so full of God, His Spirit and His Word, that there's not room for anything else!!!

8) TEACH THEM TO BECOME A PART OF A NEW TESTAMENT KINGDOM CHURCH THAT WILL DO THE WILL OF GOD UNCOMPROMISINGLY, AND TO BECOME A VITAL FUNCTIONING PART OF IT, I CORINTHIANS 14 —STYLE.

28. HAVE THEM READ STUDY & REVIEW THE MATERIAL IN THIS BOOK. HAVE THEM COMPLETE THE QUESTIONNAIRE FOUND AT THE BEGINNING OF THIS BOOK, - THEN REVIEW IT AND GO OVER IT WITH THEM.

HOW TO RAISE PERFECT KIDS!
KINGDOM PRINCIPLES
(A REVIEW)

1. If "all things are possible with God!" and if you "can do all things through Christ who strengthens" you, then it's possible to raise perfect kids!!!

2. God owns your child! God does not intend that your child "belong" to you. He wants you to dedicate your child(ren) completely to Him, so that your child is no longer yours, but His! God will in turn allow you to raise His child for Him — but He retains right of ownership in the child.

3. God intends that the home be a "corner of His Kingdom", a prototype or an example of the Kingdom of God — on earth. This means that we are not to allow anything to occur in the family or home, that is not "Kingdom" — that is, not in conformity to God's will.

4. We join or enter into the Kingdom of God, by being born again, that is, by inviting Jesus Christ into our hearts and lives to take over completely, as our Saviour, Lord, and Life!!!

5. Ministry to our spouse has a place of priority over the ministry to one's children, but God's Spirit will always lead as to priorities.

6. The Bible is the best textbook for knowing "How To Raise Perfect Kids". Therefore, it is very important that every parent reads the entire Bible through, without skipping any parts.

7. The most important thing that we can know after our initial acceptance of Christ — is the King's Greatest Secret!!! This is God's secret way to enable us to be "Purfect Parents" — Christ Himself, living in us as our very life — on location within us. Christ Himself actually being the parent of your child, through you!!!

8. It becomes accredited to our account, as having been done to Christ, the way we treat each other —our spouse, our children.

9. "Innocent until proven guilty!" We are never to punish our child unless we are absolutely sure of his or her guilt.

10. Keep in mind that the real enemy is the devil. "We wrestle not against flesh and blood, but against principalities", etc.

11. We must be always childlike, but never child-ish. Jesus said that "unless we be as little children, we cannot enter into the Kingdom of God."

12. Unconditional Love: our love for our children must never be a "performance BASED LOVE", BUT IT MUST BE UNCONDITIONAL. THIS means that we will love them, even if they choose the ways of death, destruction, and everlasting hell. God's love, and ours, requires no payment. It is freely given. A prostitute demands payment for the "love" she gives.

13. For better or for worse, our children will attribute to God, characteristics that they see in us.

14. The parent is the child's most important pastor. God gives each parent a solemn charge to raise

that child in the way of God. Therefore, it is absolutely imperative that we pray with, read to, and bless our children, as their "Pastor in the home".

15. Only say "NO" one time. We train the child that we never "mean business", until we say "NO" as many times as we normally do; and that God, the Teacher, the Policeman - doesn't mean business either. If they don't get the message the first time you say no, don't say no again, get up and teach them the fear of God! (and the flexible green switch!)

16. Use a flexible green switch. The Hebrew word for rod is "shebet" and means a "flexible switch". It stings, but doesn't bruise muscles or break cartilage.

17. Never abuse the child, either by over-diciplining or by under-disciplining, or God will discipline you!!!

18. Go through the Book of Proverbs, and note all that it has to say about raising children.

19. Don't raise your voice! You are training the child that you don't "mean business" until you do.

20. Don't threaten the child. He'll think you don't mean it until you do.

21. Always discipline to the point of repentance. Give them three licks with the switch or so, then stop and "check his spirit". If his attitude is wrong, tell him to immediately get a right spirit. If he does not, give him three more licks with the switch, and so on, until his spirit is right. By this

means, you are teaching the child two things: 1) control over his or her own spirit and attitude, and 2) quick repentance.

22. Discipline as much for a wrong reaction or attitude, as for a wrong action. After the first set of licks with the switch, you are no longer disciplining for a wrong action. From then on you are disciplining for a wrong attitude.

23. Insist that the child co-operate with you in the discipline process, even to the point of getting his own switch, etc. Teach the child that if he resists, that there will be a separate, and more severe punishment, for his failure to co-operate.

24. "Stop your crying": sometimes tears are good, but sometimes they are tears of rage, self pity, or fake. Tears of repentance are good, but do not allow tears that reflect a wrong attitude.

25. The discipline process begins at the cradle. A six-month old baby may try to manipulate you into picking him up at his whim, when in fact, the baby may need to sleep, etc. Obviously, one would not switch a baby, but we are talking about a discipline that may be as simple as not letting the baby have its own way, when it is to his own hurt.

26. Never let the child win, when he has decided to do something against what you have determined to be right for him. If you let him win at this time, it will be terrifyingly more difficult for you to bring him into line, at any time in the future.

27. Let the child win. On the other hand, let the child participate in the plan and decision making process, so that his creative initiative can be reinforced, as though he is impirtant — because he (or she) is!!!

28. Don't kill or cripple the child's spirit. Don't tell him he is no-good, lazy, or stupid. Because he loves you, he will believe you. Do not make requirements upon the child that he cannot meet, or he will give up in despair.

29. Always minister love after the discipline. Let the child know that you have forgiven, and that your love is not a "performance-based" love.

30. Treat lying as being the "worst" sin, with a much more severe and separate punishment, say, 7 to 12 licks with the switch, as opposed to the regular two or three. If you do not have a relationship of trust—there is no relationship! Besides, "liars burn in hell".

31. Dynamic dialogue with the child is imperative. Do not punish the child unless he understands why he is being punished. Quietly help him understand that obedeince to parents and God is necessary for their own benefit. Keep the channels of communication open. Have regular times of fellowhsip and "happy chats".

32. Pray together regularly as a family.

33. Have times of recreation, fun, and laughter, as a family.

34. Work together as a family. Insist that the child "carry his own load" of responsibility, without

having to be bribed, threatened or nagged. This includes, keeping clean his own room, picking up after himself, etc.; but family chores as well.

35. Respect the child's privacy.
36. Have regular "family meetings" where everyone is kept up to date with each other, discussing new business, old business, plans, problems. Especially, let this be a time of expressing gratitude to each other for the good.
37. When all else fails, practice spiritual quarantine.
38. Keep a right spirit toward your child, and generally.
39. Repent to your child if you discover that you were wrong.
40. Teach the child that the first rule in horse-play or humor is: "never have horse-play or humor if it is not fun for everyone, or if it is at someone else's EXPENSE.
41. "A little child shall lead them" the Bible says. Be willing to learn from your child, even to the point of letting God talk to you through them.
42. Sex education: teach the child, little by little, as the years go by, the facts of life, but keeping in mind a "Pandora's box" and a "do not open until marriage" mentality. "This bundle (of sexual information) is too heavy for you to carry now", a wise parent told the young daughter, "Let me carry it for you until you are old enough." Once the water is applied to the seed to be sprouted, it is difficult to reverse the process. So it is also with sexual awakening. We

encourage that these lie dormant until close to marriage.

43. Teach the child an "attitude of gratitude", as well as politeness, and consideration for others.

44. Keep your word to your child. Keep your promises. Follow through on your commitments.

45. Make sure that you do not gossip about others. It is amazing how parents are amazed at their children not walking with God later on, when earlier, they would criticize the church and ministries, not realizing how deeply the children were being affected.

46. Love: "Above all things, have fervent love for each other out of a pure heart."

47. Be best friends with your child. Cultivate and tenderly guard your relationship with your child, instilling within them early that the reason they will do the right thing, is because he chooses to, and wants to, and not because he has to. A lady was visiting in a home where a little boy lived. She said, "I'll give you a quarter if you'll be a good goy." He drew himself up tall and said, "Ma'am, I intend to be a good boy, whether you give me a quarter or not!"

48. Adventure! Cultivate within your child a zest for adventure, to not feel illegitimately compelled to be a "people pleaser".

49. Help instill within your child a large vision, seeing things from God's perspective.

50. Encourage your child to be 100% totally dedicated to God and His will for their life.

REVIEW QUESTIONS - CHAPTER 11

1. Complete the sentence: Never minister on
_____ terms, or _____ terms, but only, ever
and always, on _____ terms.
2. The first step in counseling is to get all parties to
agree on _____ .
3. Give at least three reasons why we recommend
that a man never minister alone to a woman, or a
woman to a man?
4. Why is it so important to "maintain confidence"
or secrecy in counseling?
5. Why do we have all parties in the argument
assume 100% of the responsibility for the
problem?
6. Is it possible for the parties in the relationship to
always keep a right attitude or spirit?
7. Why do we emphasize God's ability to change a
telephone pole into a good mate?
8. Why do we emphasize the 70 x 7 principle?
9. Have you ever counseled or been involved in a
situation where a relationship used up all 490 of
them in one day?
10. Why is forgiveness so important?
11. Describe the need for a referee.
12. Describe the need for "healing of the memories"
13. Point out the need for "deliverance" in
counseling.
14. Why is self confidence so important in
counseling?

15. Give at least 2 reasons for all parties to be able to take notes during counseling.
16. What does "wrestling not against flesh and blood" have to do with counseling?
17. Why is the withholding of affection a criminal offense in marriage?
18. Why the use of the "Kingdom Contract" in counseling, and where should it come in to the counseling session?

12

THE MOST IMPORTANT THING
or
GOD'S PRIORITIES
or
HAMARTANO

We have thoroughly established that it is really possible to have a "Kingdom Family" that flows and functions in a manner really pleasing to God. With God helping us, how can we do otherwise?!. For, in Christ, it really is possible to live "happily ever after"!!! For those of you who are interested in the marriage aspect of the family, please get hold of our book, *The Sexual Ministry*. Simply send a love offering to The Great Commission Ministries, P.O. 7123, Minneapolis, MN., 55407.

But now let us turn together as a family and look once again in closing at—

PRIORITIES

I used to be into gun shooting, knife throwing, archery, churiken and sling shots, etc. As a kid on the Iowa farm, we supplemented our table with rabbit and squirrel meat and we used to aim for the eye so as not to waste meat. But if we missed the target by more than an inch, then we missed the target! Guess where the expression "bull's eye" came from. But now I'm into "the weapons of our warfare" that "are MIGHTY through God!!!" Some Scriptures on this are: Sweet Psalm 149, I Cor.9:7, II Cor.10:4, & I Tim.1:18. (See also our book, *HOW TO RULE THE WORLD or SEEK 1ST THE KINGDOM OF GOD!* There were men of God who were able to hit a target and not miss "by a hair's breadth" (Judges 20:16 & I Chron.12:2.) Paul said, "Forgetting every thing else, I press towards the MARK for the PRIZE of THE HIGH CALLING of God in Christ Jesus!!!"

The most often used word for sin in the Bible is a Greek word Hamartano. (All of the a's are pronounced like, "open your mouth and say 'ah' ", emphasis on tan, and then o as in oh!) Hamartano means "to miss the mark or to miss the bull's eye!"

You know the place on the bull's eye target I hate the most? You guessed it! The part right next to the center ring! Because, if I miss the bull's eye, I've MISSED!

On the Judgement Day, we will be held responsible for only two things: 1) Did we hit the mark, or the bull's eye of the Will or Plan or Blueprint or Destiny of God for our life, and, 2) Did we do God's will for our life with a sweet spirit or a positive attitude or a right heart.

The Bible says that we are "saved" or "born again" by simply accepting Jesus Christ in to our hearts and lives to be our Lord and Saviour and Master by simply inviting Him within to take over completely to forgive all sin and give us the free gift of His Salvation from sin, selfishness, futility and hell. He actually BECOMES our Salvation! But THE REASON we become born anew IS SO THAT WE WILL DO THE PLAN & BLUEPRINT & WILL OF GOD & HIS DESTINY FOR OUR LIVES!!! Ephesians 2:8-10 says this same thing.

In other words, God has planned for us a whole life time of LIVING WORKS and CREATIVE WORDS for us to do and speak!!! Glorious Adventure! Exhilarating Thrill! Actualized Potential! Greatest Opportunity! Unsailed Seas! Uncharted Territory! Fabulous Experiences! Exciting Plans! Futility Gone! Fulfillment Fulfilled! Unexplored Explorations!

Soon, we will all be tested on how much we did of His plan for us.

THE JUDGEMENT SEAT OF CHRIST!!!

"For we must ALL appear before the Judgement Seat of Christ, That EVERYONE will receive the things done in the body, according to what you have done, whether it be good or bad. Knowing therefore, THE TERROR OF THE LORD, we persuade men..."!!! II Cor.5.

Heb.10:31 - "It is a fearful thing to fall into the hands of the Living God!!!"

Like the song goes, "FOREVER IS A LONG, LONG TIME TO BURN!!!!!"

Wise Solomon reduced it down for us to it's

simplest form. God spoke through him, "Let us hear the conclusion of the whole matter: 'Fear God, and keep His commandments: for this is the whole duty of man. For God shall bring every work into judgment, with every secret thing, whether it be good, or whether it be evil." Ecclesiastes 12:13 & 14.

We have seen how God will bring horrible judgement upon all of us who cannibalize others in the body of Christ, for IT SHALL BE ACCREDITED TO OUR ACCOUNT, AS HAVING BEEN DONE TO CHRIST, THE WAY WE RELATE TO EVEN THE LEAST OF THOSE WHO ARE DOING THE WILL OF GOD!!!

But it can be simplified even more! Master, which is the great (that is, the greatest) commandment in the law? Jesus said unto him, 'THOU SHALT LOVE THE LORD THY GOD WITH ALL THY HEART, AND WITH ALL THY SOUL, AND WITH ALL THY MIND. THIS IS THE FIRST AND GREAT(EST) COMMANDMENT And the second is like unto it, THOU SHALT LOVE THY NEIGHBOR AS THYSELF!!! ON THESE TWO COMMANDMENTS HANG ALL THE LAW AND THE PROPHETS! Matthew 23:36-40.

HELLO, MY BROTHER! HELLO, MY SISTER!

Jesus said that it will be accredited to our account, as having been done to Christ, the way we relate to even the least of His "brethren"! And who did He say that His brethren are? He said, "My mother, brother and sister is he or she that DOES THE WILL OF MY

203

FATHER!" And that's who our mother, brother or sister is today, also! (Matthew 25 & ch 12). Hello, my brother! Hello, my sister! We love you!!!

As I said to some fellow elders in an elders' meeting one time during a h'ated discussion, "Dear ones, please, there's no law against love. So please, let's just love each other!" You know what? They did not take my advice, and their church has been on a down hill slide ever since. It's really very simple isn't it.

Some folks would recommend that evangelism and testifying are the most important things, but the greatest witness of all is our love. For Jesus says, "By this shall all men know that ye are My disciples, if ye have LOVE ONE TO ANOTHER!!!" John 13:35.

REMEMBER!

Remember when Jesus said, "If you receive a little child in My Name, you receive Me..and Him Who sent Me!" Mat.18:5; Mk.9:37; Lk.9:48.

Do you remember when Jesus said, "Permit the little children to come unto Me, and forbid them not, for of such is the Kingdom Of Heaven (or the Kingdom Of God)." Mat.19:14; Mk.10:14; Lk.18:16.

Remember when Jesus said, "If you offend one of these little ones, it would be better for you than that you had a millstone hung around your neck and that you be drowned in the depths of the sea." Mat.18:6-14; Mk.9:42 Lk.17:2.

And now we conclude with this thought. It is not enough that we only tolerate or accept or like or even love each other, or these children, but the

204

commandment is given to us from God Himself in the Holy Bible, in I Peter 1:22 and 4:8. "Seeing that ye have purified your souls in obeying the Truth through the Spirit unto unfeigned love of the brethren, SEE THAT YE LOVE ONE ANOTHER WITH A PURE HEART FERVENTLY!!!" (Fervently means with white hot burning intensity)! And here is the first and the final Word:

"AND ABOVE ALL THINGS HAVE FERVENT LOVE AMONG YOURSELVES."

Dear Heavenly Father, we know that You shall always be our Father, and that we shall always be Your children. Thank You Dear Heavenly Daddy, for loving us so faithfully. Help us to always rightly relate to these Your children in a manner well pleasing to Thee. We know that You, Lord, are great enough to teach us, and enable us by Thy grace, through Thy power, by Thy Life lived through us to know — **HOW TO RAISE PERFECT CHILDREN!!!**

In Jesus Name. Amen.

REVIEW QUESTIONS - CHAPTER 12

1. Please complete this Kingdom Principle, "It is accredited to our account, as having been done to _____ ."

2. On what commandments can be "hung" all of the law and all of the prophets?

3. Jesus said that by what would "all men know that you are" His disciples?

4. I Peter says that we are to love each other how?

5. Do you believe that it is possible to raise perfect children?

EPILOGUE

AND THE HUMPTY DUMPTY HEARTS
LIVED HAPPILY EVER AFTER

A man of God once said to us through his tears, "Listen, can you hear them crying?" He was talking one Sunday Morning about the hearts and souls that were still hurting from the night before. I have worked now for several years as a counsellor for the CBN 700 Club "Love Lines". The first call I got was from a teen age girl who had just taken apparently a whole bottle of "red devils", or seconal, and was just calling to say 'good bye' to someone just before she died. Fortunately, we were able to trace the call and get to her in time. Another true story tells of a person who was walking onto a bridge where they planned to end it "Humpty Dumpty" style. But as he (or she) was walking onto the bridge, they were passed by a born again Christian who simply smiled and said, "hello", and walked on by. That Christian's smile alone caused a realization that life was not entirely hopeless and that Humpty Dumpty friend changed his mind, found Christ, later met the person with the smile, and they lived happily ever after!

Have you ever been lonely? It's a strange thing indeed, that sometimes the most unloveable, need love the most. Our Lord talks about a wonderful ministry we are all called to be a part of — A sweet sweet ministry of God's love — to Help Heal Hurting Humpty Dumpty hearts!!! Have you ever been lonely, lonely even in a crowd? Has your heart of emotion ever hurt so bad you thought it would tear out your throat? You are called to the most wonderful ministry of all — the ministry of encouragement to others. Our commission from the Lord Jesus and the Loving Heart of the Heavenly Father is that we can "comfort others with the Love with which we have been comforted."

GOD HAS A VISION
WE HAVE A VISION
I HAVE A VISION
PLEASE, HAVE OUR VISION

God's vision is to see the Gospel of the Kingdom preached to the uttermost part of the world. The desire of our hearts for this book is to open opportunities to present the Good News of Kingdom of God principles to those who would present the Good News of the Kingdom of God, ect... As the

Apostle Paul said, "The things that you have learned and received from Me, commit thou to faithful men, who will be able to teach others, also."

Would you seek God? Would you seek God very earnestly? Would you seek God from your heart to see whether or not you will share this vision? Would you seek God deep in your heart to make God's vision YOUR VISION?

As we have stated before, our whole desire is to do God's will.

If we can be of any help, in any way that will promote the Kingdom of God on earth, please call on us. Our present address is on the back cover of this book. We thank God for the response to His Divine Call to the Dynamic Destiny of Discipleship!!!

There are available to you representatives of the Kingdom of God to come to your area for classes, seminars, sermons, on more than the following areas, including the material taught in this book: Marriage and family, Discipleship training, the Lordship of Christ, the Fullness of God, Church Growth and Renewal, The KINGDOM OF GOD.

THE GREAT COMMISSION

The God of all Heaven and Earth speaks to you now, a crystal clear, pure and sure, thus saith the Lord Yahweh:

"SEEK YE FIRST THE KINGDOM OF GOD,
AND HIS RIGHTEOUSNESS;
AND ALL THESE THINGS
WILL BE ADDED UNTO YOU!!!" "GO YE THEREFORE
AND TEACH [MAKE DISCIPLES OF]
ALL NATIONS,
BAPTIZING THEM IN THE
NAME OF THE FATHER,
AND OF THE SON,
AND OF THE HOLY GHOST." "TEACHING THEM TO OBEY ALL THINGS WHATSOEVER I HAVE COMMANDED YOU.
AND LO, I AM WITH YOU ALWAYS,
EVEN UNTO THE END OF THE WORLD."
AMEN.

KINGDOM QUESTIONS
(PLEASE RESPOND)

1. Do you know of anyone that could benefit from any part of the Kingdom of God in terms of counselling, prayer, training, personal ministry, visitation, encouragement, seminars or additional copies of this book, etc.?

2. Do you know of any source that has abilities or resources they would like to volunteer for the cause of the advancement of the Gospel of the Kingdom?

3. Do you personally have any needs the Kingdom of God could meet such as prayer, encouragement, counselling, fellowship, books, seminars, commissioning, training, etc.?

4. Do you personally have any gifts or abilities, time or talents, money or possessions that you would be willing to volunteer to the cause of Christ as it relates to the Kingdom of God and to the spreading of the Gospel of the Kingdom? On a short term basis; or long term; or monthly basis?

5. Do you know of any group or church that could benefit in any way from the resources of the Kingdom of God in terms of retreats, conferences, meetings, seminars, teaching, Bible studies, speakers, etc.?, on the subjects of

Discipleship-Leadership Training, Church Growth and Renewal, Marriage and Family, etc.?

6. Do you have any constructive counsel for this presentation? Other ideas for the outreach of the Gospel of the Kingdom? Anything to offer that would be of help?

7. Would you be interested in fellowship or getting to know others that also have an unreserved discipleship commitment to Jesus Christ the Lord and King?

8. Are you willing to give and live your life completely to the King of Kings, and Lord of lords, to seek first the Kingdom of God and His righteousness?

9. Has this book been a blessing to you? We would like to know.

10. Would you be interested in contributing or helping to get this book into the hands of those not able to pay for it, i.e., the poor, "shut-in's," prisoners, other countries, students, hospitalized, etc.?

11. Do you know of anyone who would like this book on tape or in another language?

12. Would you like a copy or copies of the Kingdom Contract evangelism brochure?

13. Would you like to have additional copies of this book? It was designed for use in any of the

following ways: Seminary, Bible College, Bible School, Sunday School, Seminars, Conferences, Church Renewal, Discipleship-Leadership Training, Personal Study, Family Devotions, Home Meetins, Classroom Curriculum, Men's Women's, Children's Meetings, Sermon or Teaching Series, publication in periodicals, etc.

14. Would you like to be kept informed of new books or developments relating to the ministry of the Great Commission?

All correspondence may be directed to:
The Great Commission Ministries
c/o John Bohlen
P.O. Box 7123
Minneapolis, Minnesota 55407

This book is also available on tape cassettes.

(All gifts to The Great Commission Ministries are tax deductible.)

OPPORTUNITY!

You can help fulfill the Great Commission through book sales and distribution, along with other Christian Bibles, books, tapes, and records, while at the same time obtaining your own material at a discount or for profit to you and your organization.

If you cannot afford to pay for these products please let us know so we can look to the Lord together to see if we can work something out. O.K.???!!!

Great Commission Ministries
P.O. Box 7123
Minneapolis, Minnesota 55407

All profits from this book, or contributions, are used for the fulfillment of the Great Commission.

BOOK & PRICE LIST

Books or Pamphlets by John Roy Bohlen & JOHN 5:30

"How To Rule The World"	Available now
"Cult of Cannibals"	Available now
"The Sexual Ministry"	Available now
"How To Raise 'Purfect' Kids"	Available Now

Seminar Video Cassette 8 hrs. $50.00 on
How To Rule The World

Pamphlets:
> "The King's Greatest Secret"
> " $$"
> "Hell! Forever Is A Long Loooooooong
> Time To Burn!"

Cassette Tapes:
> "Helping Heal Hurting Humpty-Dumpty Hearts"
> "The King's Greatest Secret"
> "How To Rule The World"
> "Discipleship Training Seminar"
> The sound track of the video tape.

If you cannot afford these materials, we will work with you.

GOD'S SWEET BEST TO YOU!